The New RAYBURN Cookbook

The New
RAYBURN
Cookbook

Richard Maggs and Dawn Roads

RAYBURN

A.
Absolute Press

First published in Great Britain in 2005
by Absolute Press, an imprint of
Bloomsbury Publishing

Absolute Press
Scarborough House
29 James Street West
Bath BA1 2BT
Phone 44 (0) 1225 316013
Fax 44 (0) 1225 445836
E-mail office@absolutepress.co.uk
Website www.absolutepress.co.uk

Reprinted
2007, 2009, 2010, 2011, 2013, 2014

Bloomsbury Publishing Plc
50 Bedford Square
London WC1B 3DP
www.bloomsbury.com

Bloomsbury is a trademark of
Bloomsbury Publishing Plc.

Publisher Jon Croft
Editor Meg Avent
Design Matt Inwood & Maria Bowers

Photographer Andy Davies
Home Economist Tina Boughey

A catalogue record of this book is available
from the British Library.

ISBN 9781904573265

Printed in China by C&C Offset Printing Co., Ltd.

CONTENTS

INTRODUCTION

The Rayburn is a legendary British invention which has been warming homes and providing outstanding cooking for more than fifty years. The castings are still made at the historic Coalbrookdale foundry in Ironbridge, birthplace of the industrial revolution.

THE RAYBURN – IT'S A WAY OF LIFE

Quite apart from the superlative cooking that's so easy to achieve on the Rayburn, it is the gentle warm presence the cooker provides that turns your kitchen into the very heart of your home.

Whether you have a traditional or rapid response model, the versatility of the Rayburn quite simply makes life easier. Whether this means cooking food fast or cooking food slow, cooking for one person, or for many, the flexibility of the spacious ovens and generous hotplate means everything is possible.

Every Rayburn installation varies slightly, depending on model, fuel and flue choice. Provided the cooker is correctly installed in accordance with Rayburn's installation recommendations, this book will help you to get the very best from of your cooker.

A comprehensive operating instructions booklet is supplied with every new Rayburn. This shows how to control your model, and how to regulate the cooker to the desired oven setting. This book is generic to all Rayburns and should be read in conjunction with the operating instructions booklet for your model. If you have inherited your Rayburn, please contact Rayburn direct for a replacement copy of the operating instructions.

We have both cooked on Rayburns for many years and hope that you enjoy trying out our recipes, old and new. We have really enjoyed writing this book together and hope that you have many happy years ahead cooking with your Rayburn.

RICHARD MAGGS AND DAWN ROADS

HOW TO USE THIS BOOK

We hope that this book will help you to quickly understand how to get the very best from your Rayburn. The main principles have been kept as simple as possible.

For oven temperatures and positioning, each recipe follows a standard format. In some cases there is an alternative slow oven cooking option which is only for models which feature a Cast-Iron Lower Oven. Where this is the case, this alternative option is shown with the symbol **Ⓒ**. In the example below, the first line shows the standard cooking method that is possible with all models. The Main Oven should be brought to 120°C (250°F), Gas Mark L-1. Consult the operating instructions booklet for your model for details on how to regulate your Rayburn to obtain this setting. If you have a Cast-Iron Lower Oven, as an alternative this oven could be used for the same time, in Slow Cooking Mode. This is achieved with the Main Oven set at 200°C (400°F), Gas Mark 6 or above. In a few other recipes involving long simmering, an alternative hotplate method is also given as an alternative.

MAIN OVEN 120°C (250°F), GAS MARK L-1 [Standard method for ALL models]

Ⓒ LOWER OVEN IN SLOW COOKING [Mode Alternative method for Cast Iron Lower Oven models ONLY]

Recipes suitable for vegetarians have been flagged with the symbol .

HOW THE RAYBURN WORKS

The Rayburn is a semi heat-storage cooker. From the original solid fuel model introduced in 1946 to the very latest models, the simple principles on which they operate have reassuringly remained the same. A comparatively small and efficient heat source radiates and conducts heat to the different parts of the cooker, and a single cooker control regulates the heat. In this way the hotplate and ovens are given a steady supply of heat in different proportions, making constant regulation largely unnecessary.

Traditional models are designed to be operated continuously – overnight and between meals when little or no cooking is required, the cooker is turned down to its lowest setting to run at an idling setting. Some time before cooking, the controls should be adjusted, as required, to allow a build up of heat ready for cooking. The time it takes to bring the cooker from an idling setting to a moderate oven is 20-40 minutes, depending on model.

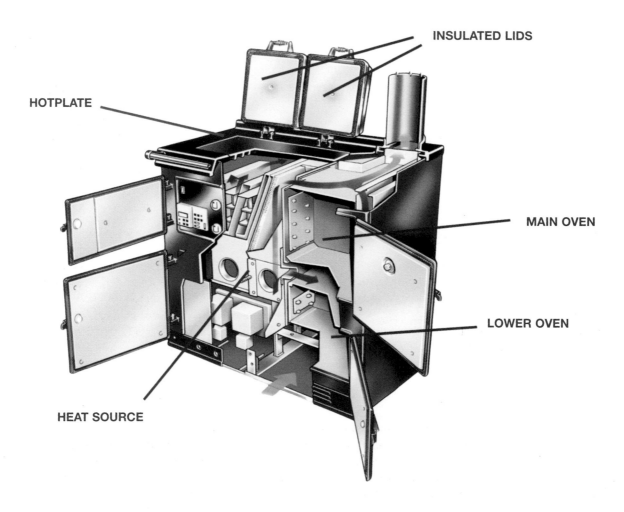

INSULATED LIDS

HOTPLATE

MAIN OVEN

LOWER OVEN

HEAT SOURCE

The rapid response models can also be operated, if required, at an idling setting. Alternatively, this type can be turned off completely when not required. The burner design in this type of Rayburn provides the fastest heat-up of all; heating a moderate oven from cold in as little as 20-30 minutes, with the hotplate useable in an even shorter time. Most models can be programmed to turn on automatically making them ready for immediate use on your return home after work.

As the hotplate and ovens both receive a share of the heat from the burner, they will vary in temperature depending on setting. Simply move food to a hotter or cooler position to fine-tune the rate of cooking. Cast iron retains heat superbly for a long time, helped by the efficient insulation which is packed within the cooker. The Main Oven in particular holds its heat for a long time after the cooker has been turned down. You will soon find simple ways to use this energy. Suggestions of how to use this stored heat are given throughout this book.

The ovens on all models are vented to the outside, so cooking smells are taken away from the kitchen helping to keep the cooking environment clean and fresh. We recommend you invest in a timer to remind you that something is cooking, and pop a Post-it note or an oven-reminder magnet on the door to prevent any chance of forgetting.

CONTROLLING YOUR RAYBURN

COOKER CONTROL
Depending on model, your Rayburn will have manual or thermostatic controls. Both types are easy to regulate – for exact details refer to the operating instructions booklet for your particular cooker as the instructions vary from model to model. On rapid response models the control on the front of the cooker is calibrated in Gas Marks, 1-9. Some traditional models have a side control positioned low down which is calibrated 1-6 to cover the same temperature range. On others the side control is positioned higher up and is calibrated in degrees Celsius or Fahrenheit. Solid and multi-fuel models require manual manipulation of the draught spin-wheel and flue damper.

CENTRAL HEATING AND HOT WATER CONTROL
Where central heating and/or hot water are provided by your Rayburn, on most traditional models a single burner provides heat for cooking and hot water, so the higher the cooker setting, the more hot water is produced. Where a second burner is provided this is used separately to provide central heating. On rapid response models two independent burners are provided, each dedicated to its specific task. The cooker burner provides heat for the hotplate and ovens, whilst a second burner separately provides heat for hot water and central heating, as required. Most models can also be controlled with an electronic programmer so that you can set the heating and cooker to come on independently in anticipation of your return home, providing total control to suit modern lifestyles.

THE THERMODIAL

The Thermodial oven temperature gauge on the Main Oven door gives an indication of the centre oven temperature. It should only be read when the door has not been recently opened as the temperature will appear to drop once the door is opened. Simply close the door and after a few minutes the true temperature can be read again. You will find that exact temperatures are less critical compared to conventional cookers. Set the controls to obtain the recommended temperatures and position the food accordingly – if you use a shelf position a little higher or lower than suggested, the food will simply cook slightly faster or more slowly.

RAYBURN CAST-IRON COOKING
GETTING THE BEST FROM YOUR RAYBURN

THE HOTPLATE

The heavy cast-iron hotplate is machine ground completely flat to make perfect contact with kettles and saucepans for efficient heat transfer. It is graduated in temperature from fast boiling on one side across to gentle simmering on the other – this configuration varies according to model. Simply slide pans across the hotplate depending on whether boiling or simmering is required. The overall hotplate temperature is adjusted by the cooker control.

If your cooker is idling and you need the hotplate to be hotter, simply advance the control for a period. For a quick response, for instance to boil a kettle first thing in the morning, turn the control to a high setting and put the kettle onto the boiling end of the hotplate. Once boiled, an appropriate setting can then be selected according to immediate cooking needs. If the oven is not needed at a high temperature reduce to a lower setting. Boiling of kettles, vegetables and jam for a set will be faster when the cooker is at a high setting. This is also important for stir-frying in an Aga Wok (*see* p15) and for deep-fat frying (pre-heat on the simmering end first). For all sustained high-temperature cooking, the fastest results are achieved when the cooker is on a rising heat. From experience you will quickly find which settings are most convenient for your needs.

To get the best results it is important to use cookware with thick and perfectly flat bases (*see* p14) – these ensure good contact and even and efficient heat conduction. Pans with thick bases will continue to boil even if they are only partly on the hotplate – the hotplate is fitted slightly proud of the top plate to enable you to partially offset pans to regulate the rate of cooking, without damaging the enamel top plate.

Bread, teacakes and crumpets can be toasted by placing these directly onto the hotplate. For toast that does not stick, the hotplate should be at least at a moderate temperature – cook directly on the simmering end or middle, depending on setting. The hotplate should always be kept absolutely clean, so use a wire brush afterwards as otherwise toast crumbs will prevent efficient heat transfer to pans, meaning they will not boil as quickly.

When at a moderate temperature, the simmering end can also be used as a griddle. Toasted sandwiches also cook perfectly here, either directly on the hotplate, or on a piece of Bake-O-Glide (*see* p15). When not in use, always keep the insulated lids down on the hotplate to conserve heat, even if only for a few minutes.

THE TOP PLATE
WARMING AND DRYING ITEMS

You will find that the gentle warmth on the top plate is invaluable for warming and drying things such as awkward-shaped metal cooking utensils and kitchen gadgets. Small containers of jam, syrup or butter may be warmed or melted for easy spreading or pouring. Place a Pyrex bowl on the top plate to make and keep hot delicate sauces such as Hollandaise and Béarnaise. Teapots, sauceboats and vegetable tureen lids can also be warmed here before use.

KEEPING COOKED FOOD HOT

The top plate is invaluable when cooking a large roast meal. It's where the cooked meat or poultry can be kept hot in a clean meat tin, covered with foil, while vegetables and trimmings are finished off in the ovens with the cooker turned to a high setting. To prevent damage to the enamel: always place items on a folded piece of kitchen paper or Rayburn chef's pad. Always use a chef's pad or folded cloth on the closed lids if using them for keeping food hot. Some power flue models have an extra feature of a warming plate at the back right of the top plate which is ideal for keeping a coffee pot warm.

IDLING WARMTH FOR OFF-PEAK WARMING

The warmth from the Rayburn top plate when the cooker is at a low setting is useful for warming mixing bowls with bread flour (the finished dough is best proved on the worktop next to the cooker). Place bowls on a cork mat on the top plate when making yoghurt overnight or for slightly softening butter for spreading and for gently melting chocolate.

THE MAIN OVEN

The large Main Oven is made of cast iron and is indirectly heated by conduction, radiation and convection. This means an exceptionally even, all-round heat and depending on setting, this oven acts as a roasting, baking and simmering oven. With no naked flames or elements in the oven, full use can be made of the whole cooking space. Its cast-iron construction helps produce the perfect roast, sealing in all the juices and flavour. It's also large enough to accommodate a 13kg (28 lb) turkey. The oven runners will take the grid and plain shelves as well as the meat tin and they are counted downwards from one to five.

When the Thermodial registers a setting, this is a guide to the centre oven temperature. The top of the oven is a little hotter, with the area below centre a little cooler, thus providing different heat zones so that a variety of different foods can be cooked at the same time. The very coolest part of the oven is to be found as low down as possible, without making direct contact on the floor of the oven.

When the oven is hot, the floor of the oven can be used as an extra cooking surface – think of it as a hidden hotplate. It can be used for shallow-frying (a cast-iron frying pan or dish is recommended), with the advantage that fat splashes are carbonised, so cleaning is minimised. Similarly there is no need to bake pastry cases 'blind', just place the flan dish, complete with the filling, directly on the oven floor for a beautifully crisp pastry base. This also works brilliantly with fruit pies and pizzas – both bought and home-made – they will cook to perfection here. Lifting the lids on the hotplate or prolonged use of the hotplate will not affect the Main Oven temperature.

When the Main Oven is at a low or idling setting it is perfect for long slow cooking. *See* 'Off-peak cooking', p12, for suggestions.

When a very hot oven is needed for roasting, baking bread or pastry, allow up to an hour for traditional models to heat from an idling setting to the required heat. Rapid response models reach this temperature in 20-30 minutes. You will find that it is easy to cook several foods at the same time with no confusion of flavours as the oven is vented, thus allowing cooking smells to disappear to the outside.

For perfect baking results, turn food once during cooking. If you are cooking other foods that require a high setting at the same time, place cakes and biscuits lower in the oven with a cold plain shelf above, if necessary, to reduce top heat and prevent over-browning.

The top of a hot oven is where oven grilling takes place; use the meat tin with a grill rack set in the high position so that the fat can drip into the tin.

THE LOWER OVEN

The Lower Oven on your model will be one of two types. Refer to your operating instructions booklet to determine which you have, as they are used differently and operate at different temperatures.

CAST-IRON LOWER OVENS

The cast-iron cooking oven operates at around half the temperature of the Main Oven. When the Main Oven is set at 200°C (400°F), Gas Mark 6 or higher, the Lower Oven is invaluable for slow cooking casseroles and steaming vegetables, potatoes, rice and puddings (up to four pans can be stacked together to cook at the same time). Think of it as a 'continuation oven' – foods started off elsewhere in the cooker are transferred here to finish cooking. This oven is particularly useful when preparing a lot of food, as dishes that require lower temperatures can be cooked at the same time as the hot main oven. A roast can finish cooking below and the cooker control turned to a high setting for roast vegetables and trimmings to be cooked in quantity in the hot oven above. Naturally this oven can also be used for heating plates and serving dishes, keeping meals warm for late-comers and for many other uses.

STEEL LOWER OVENS

The Warming Oven found on all other models operates at around a third of the temperature of the Main Oven. It's perfect for heating plates and serving dishes, for resting joints of meat before carving and for keeping cooked food hot and plated meals warm. Because food can be kept hot here without deteriorating, it is an invaluable oven to have when cooking a large and complicated meal. Although it is not intended as a cooking oven, it is perfect for drying out meringues and herbs. Certain foods can be finished off here, such as meringue-topped desserts and fruit compôtes. The gentle heat is also perfect for drying fruit and vegetables such as for making home-made sun-dried style tomatoes. On solid fuel models this oven is slightly hotter than on other models when the cooker is at a high setting.

OFF-PEAK COOKING

This is one of the great advantages of cooking with a Rayburn, as it saves time and makes best use of your fuel. You can bring soups, curries and casseroles to the boil on the hotplate and then transfer them to continue to cook very slowly in the Main Oven at a low setting. Rich fruit cakes can be cooked long and slow, and milk puddings taste even better cooked this way (the secret of creamy rice pudding – put it in early and allow it to cook the whole morning through, *see* p112).

Baked custards, shortbread and meringues need long, gentle cooking and can be cooked in an idling oven. Inexpensive cuts of meat have a great depth of flavour and are rendered meltingly tender if you cook them slowly over a long period. Pot roasts, for instance, can be even tastier than oven roasts when cooked this way because all their flavour is locked in. Hotpots and stews will be tender and retain all their rich juices. Root vegetables can be left to cook in a tightly covered saucepan with a little stock and used to make nutritious soups that will taste absolutely delicious. Simple everyday stock from a leftover chicken carcass can be made over several hours, or creamy Rayburn porridge can be made overnight and will be ready for the whole family first thing in the morning. Many Rayburn owners who keep chickens use their idling Rayburn oven to cook kitchen scraps ready to mix with their layer's mash feed for the most economical poultry-keeping.

OFF-PEAK WARMING

The Lower Oven in all models serves as a gentle warming oven when the cooker is at a low setting. You will soon find other uses for this oven as well as merely keeping plates hot, useful as this is. So gentle is the heat that a cooked meal will stay hot for several hours without spoiling or drying up. A covered pan of hot bedtime drinks will stay hot until the last member of the family is ready for bed. Cereals, biscuits, and foods that need crisping up can be put into the warming oven. You can make rusks, or crisp bread crusts for making into breadcrumbs or to add to dog meal. Within weeks will find many other uses for the gentle, safe off-peak warmth of this oven.

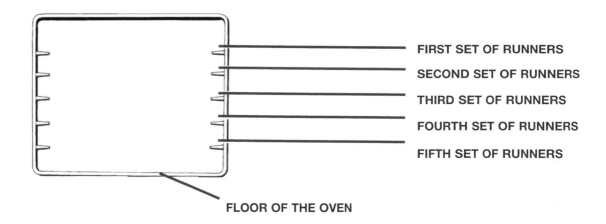

FIRST SET OF RUNNERS

SECOND SET OF RUNNERS

THIRD SET OF RUNNERS

FOURTH SET OF RUNNERS

FIFTH SET OF RUNNERS

FLOOR OF THE OVEN

RAYBURN ACCESSORIES AND COOKWARE

The oven grid shelves are designed to be non-tilt and should be fitted with the up-stands facing upwards at the back, so when pulled forward the shelf cannot come right out.

THE COLD PLAIN SHELF
The plain oven shelf has two functions, for both of these it should be used cold. For this reason this shelf should always be stored out of the oven. Firstly, it can be used as a baking sheet for foods such as rolls, scones, biscuits, etc. Secondly, it can be used as a shield to protect food placed beneath it. If the oven is too hot or food is beginning to over-brown, slide it in on the top set of runners or two runners above the food to reduce top heat and act as a shield to protect the food below it. The closer the shelf is placed to the top of the food the paler the top of the food will be.

THE MEAT TIN
The meat tin supplied with your Rayburn (except the Regent) exactly fits the oven size, hanging directly from the runners, leaving the grid shelves free for other dishes. It is also useful for cooking traybake recipes and large quantities of lasagne and shepherd's pie when feeding crowds. It will accommodate a 13kg (28 lb) turkey and other large joints of meat and poultry.

THE GRILL RACK
This accessory is designed to be used with the meat tin. Place in the high position for grilling bacon, sausages and flat fish at the top of the Main Oven, and in the low position for roasting meat and poultry. It also serves as a useful cake-cooling rack.

COOKWARE POINTERS – CORRECT BASES ESSENTIAL

It is essential that kettles and saucepans used on the Rayburn have suitable bases. A good pan with a heavy and perfectly flat base is essential. Heat is only efficiently transferred by conduction when direct contact is made with the surface of the hotplate. If utensils with a poor base are used only a few points on the base will receive heat resulting in uneven heating. This will cause slow boiling, making control difficult and giving frustratingly poor performance.

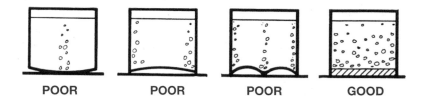

POOR   POOR   POOR   GOOD

Therefore, to get the best result it is important to use utensils that have thick and perfectly flat bases so that they make good contact. Pans need to have 6mm ($^1/_4$ inch) thick bases so that over many years of use they will not warp or distort. The bases also need to be precision finished to make the all-important direct contact across the whole of their bases for the most efficient transfer of heat. Provided your existing saucepans have heavy and perfectly flat bases, they should also give good results on your Rayburn. If you have a model with a cast-iron Lower Oven, you should aim to introduce some pans in your collection that feature recessed knobs in flat lids as these enable stacking up to four pans in this oven. Wooden handles are not suitable as they cannot be used in the ovens.

KETTLES

After much testing (and many cups of tea later!) we have reached the conclusion that a good aluminium kettle boils quickest. Modern types are available in hard anodised or plain aluminium with a non-stick internal coating. If you have aggressive water or prefer an alternative, select a stainless steel kettle. Choose one with a broad base for more contact with the hotplate.

CAST-IRON TRIVETS

Enamelled cast-iron trivets are really useful; use one to park your hot kettle. They are also invaluable for protecting work surfaces from hot trays.

AGA CAST-IRON GRILL PAN

A ridged cast-iron grill pan can be used on the hotplate for grilling steak, chops and cutlets. With the cooker at a high setting, pre-heat the dry pan on the simmering end of the hotplate for a couple of minutes. Then move it to the boiling end for 3-4 minutes before using, so that it absorbs the full amount of heat ready for cooking. Brush the ridges with a little fat from the side of the meat or very lightly oil the food, but never the pan. Place lightly on the ridges and cook to your liking, turning once. If preferred, to save mess, once the food has been placed in the pan it may be transferred to finish grilling on the floor of the oven. This pan can also be used for cooking chicken fillets, pork loin steaks and floured liver. With care you can also cook sardines and scallops and 'meatier' types of fish such as salmon, swordfish and marlin. For other fish and fillets use the top of the Main Oven on a grill rack (*see* 'Fish and Seafood' chapter).

CAST-IRON CASSEROLES

We prefer the oval type as they make the best use of space when in the ovens for slow cooking. Pre-frying of ingredients can be carried out on the hotplate before other ingredients are added, which certainly saves on washing up. The Danish Pot is brilliant – an absolute gem. Use it to make a quick rustic soup from surplus vegetables cooked with stock. A wand blender can then be used to purée it in the pan, saving on washing up.

CAST-IRON BAKING AND GRATIN DISHES

These are so versatile and ideal for preparing baked supper dishes such as chicken fillets with a sauce or sautéed diced cooked potatoes. Being enamelled, they are smart enough for the table and are perfect for serving different delicious vegetable gratins, braised vegetables and layered potato dishes.

GENERAL SAUCEPANS AND CASSEROLES

Broad-based utensils make for efficient heating as their large surface area make the best contact with the hotplate. If you want pans that can be washed in a dishwasher, the stainless steel range is the one for you. Hard anodised aluminium pans will give slightly faster boiling times, however, they are not suitable for washing in the dishwasher. The cast aluminium frying and sauté pans are great with excellent non-stick linings and the removable handles means that they can be transferred to the ovens to continue cooking.

PRESSURE COOKERS

A pressure cooker may be used on the hotplate if it has a heavy and perfectly flat base. Once brought to pressure on the boiling end, move to the other end of the hotplate to maintain the pressure – it may be necessary to partially offset the pan to give the merest thread of heat required.

RAYBURN WOK

The best wok that we have tested for the Rayburn is the Aga hard anodised aluminium wok. Pre-heat it on the simmering end of the hotplate for a couple of minutes with the cooker at a high setting. Then transfer to the boiling end for a further couple of minutes, and when really hot add the oil and get cooking.

BAKEWARE

Most good quality bakeware is fine in the Rayburn. Choose those that are heavily made and can withstand high temperatures

BAKE-O-GLIDE

Bake-O-Glide is a reusable non-stick coated cooking liner. Available in a range of packs, the Rayburn Cook Set is the most versatile. It contains pre-cut pieces to fit the meat tin and cold plain shelf. The 1 metre roll is also useful for cutting pieces to fit your favourite bakeware. It can also be used on the simmering end of the hotplate for toasting sandwiches, which makes cleaning up much easier. Although it can be used for drop scones, we prefer the finish you get when these are cooked directly on the hotplate. However, if you are using a solid fuel model, it may be useful to use the liner, as it will then cover the circular removable flue-cleaning plug in the simmering end of the hotplate. Bake-O-Glide may be washed by hand or machine – anchor it in the lower basket between two plates. Be careful not to cut it with a sharp knife, as this will damage the surface.

GAUNTLETS, OVEN GLOVES AND CHEF'S PADS

To protect your arms from a glancing burn from the sides of the oven, choose from the extensive range available. Chef's pads are great for protecting the insulated lids and as useful pot grabs.

TAKING CARE OF YOUR COOKER

The tough vitreous enamel finish on your Rayburn is extremely hard wearing but should still be treated with care. In essence it is a glass coating fused onto the cast iron under extremely high temperatures – several coats are used. We would recommend when placing things on the top plate to always protect the enamel by using a piece of folded kitchen paper, a chef's pad or a cork mat.

CLEANING AND SERVICING

CLEANING

One of the biggest assets of a Rayburn is that cleaning it is so easy. A wire brush should be used to keep the hotplate clear of carbonised food, crumbs and any other mess. This will ensure that the base of your pans continue to make perfect contact with the hotplate. General cleaning is best carried out when the Rayburn is cool. Proprietary oven cleaners are not suitable and the Rayburn range of enamel and metal cleaners is recommended, as they have been specifically developed for cast-iron range cookers.

HOW TO KEEP YOUR RAYBURN CLEAN

• Keep a damp cloth handy while you are cooking to wipe up any spills as they occur, this prevents them becoming hard and more difficult to remove later. It is important to wipe up milk, fruit juice or anything containing acid immediately, otherwise the enamel may become permanently discoloured.

• In the Main Oven, spills and fat splashes are carbonised at a high temperature, and so all that is required is an occasional brushing out with a stiff brush when the cooker is cool or switched off. On most models the oven doors can be removed for cleaning. Use gauntlets to carefully lift the door off its hinges, lay it enamel-side down on a towel to protect the enamel on the worktop. Take care to keep any plastic washers in place. Leave to cool, then clean with an approved enamel cleaner. Do not immerse in water as the doors contain insulation. Grid shelves should be soaked and stubborn spills removed with a cream cleanser. The Lower Oven can be wiped with a damp cloth to remove spills.

• The hotplate will carbonise any food or fat spilt on it and a strong wire brush should be used to keep the hotplate scrupulously clean.

• To clean the vitreous enamel; use Rayburn enamel cleaner or an approved vitreous enamel cleaner. Do not use this on stainless steel or chrome lids. The vitreous enamel finish of the Rayburn is hard wearing and to keep it looking at its best avoid dragging pans across the enamelled top plate or banging heavy pans down on the surface. Remember to wipe off any marks which may run down from the firebox after refueling on solid fuel models. For stubborn spills a wet soap-impregnated wire wool pad may be used with light pressure. Polish up with a clean dry cloth.

• Stainless steel and chrome lids and other parts – use Rayburn metal cleaner applied with a soapy cloth followed by a gentle buffing with a soft towel.

• If your Rayburn has a matt vitreous enamel finish (such as the MF multi fuel model), the cleaning procedure is slightly different. Due to the characteristics of this finish a cloth may leave lint deposits. Instead use a sponge for cleaning, with a little liquid soap or Swarfega. Hardened or burnt-on grease can be removed with a soap-impregnated pad – wipe carefully with a damp sponge to remove any wire wool particles, then finish with a little liquid soap or Swarfega on a clean damp sponge.

• With gas and oil models, periodically check behind the burner door for any accumulation of dust and fluff. Lightly brush clear.

• When your Rayburn is switched off ready for its service; take the opportunity to treat it to a complete clean, as cleaning a cold cooker is much easier.

SERVICING

Look after your Rayburn and it will look after you. To keep your cooker running efficiently it's recommended that you have it regularly serviced by an approved service engineer at the appropriate service intervals. Turn the cooker off the night before the engineer's visit as a hot cooker cannot be properly serviced.

ENJOY YOUR RAYBURN!

GOOD FOOD FAST

Good Food Fast is the section to turn to at times when life in the fast lane seems more hectic than usual. Following these recipes will enable you to cook quick, tasty and nutritious meals, instead of having the ubiquitous take-away.

READY-PREPARED FOODS

The array of good quality, ready-prepared foods and meals that are available now is immense and can rescue us mid-week, when time is at a premium with work and school activities. The Rayburn can cook several ready-meals at once, allowing each member of the family to enjoy their favourite. Place the separate containers on the plain shelf and slide into the Main Oven. The Rayburn is very accommodating as the oven is zoned in heat, so dishes requiring different temperatures can be cooked in the oven at the same time. The selected cooker setting refers to the centre of the oven, above is slightly hotter and below is slightly cooler, by around 10°C (25°F), or one Gas Mark either way. The cold plain shelf can be used as a heat deflector to protect food placed below it.

PIZZA

Ready-prepared meals, such as pizza, can be enhanced by being cooked in the Rayburn.
The cast-iron oven is indirectly heated and so radiates heat from all sides, including the oven floor. Indeed, the Rayburn has been likened to a pizza wood oven, or a bakers' brick oven. A pizza can be unwrapped and zapped on the floor of a hot Main Oven and cooked really quickly It will emerge after a few minutes with a crisp base and melted topping. Serve with a salad to complete the meal.

SAUCES

Adding ready-made sauces to a recipe can save time, for example, oven-roasted salmon (*see* p61) with a carton of dill sauce added can be ready in just a few minutes. Pasta can be cooked on the boiling side of the hotplate and served with a ready-made puttanesca sauce. Gnocchi smothered in a ready-made blue cheese sauce with grated cheese topping can be put together and oven cooked within half an hour. However, 'ready-prepared' need not mean commercially made, you can produce your own meals and sauces with the use of the freezer for storage. During a cooking session just make double quantities, one for now and one for later.

PASTRY

One real boon we have found is the new type of ready-rolled shortcrust pastry now available which lines a 20cm (8 inch) flan dish – excellent for a quick quiche or tart. Also, ready-rolled puff pastry is wonderful for dishes such as, Goats' Cheese, Tomato and Basil Tartlets, (*see* p82) or for beef or salmon en croûte.

Home-made pastry can be frozen at the 'rubbed in stage' so you can take it straight from the freezer, mix with water and use. Another way is to line flan tins with pastry, freeze, and then bake from frozen. Cooking from frozen means no baking beans are required. Brilliant for recipes, such as, Lemon Meringue Pie, (*see* p109), which usually require baking blind before adding the filling. Alternatively, fill the frozen pastry case with a sweet or savoury filling and bake directly on the floor of the oven.

Another good food fast tip is to make up a quantity of crumble topping and then place in the freezer to be used at a moment's notice, for a quick fruit dessert or a streusel topping.

CHICKEN ROCKS

A healthier and larger version of the chicken 'nugget'!

SERVES 4
12-16 mini chicken fillets
2 tbsp butter
115g (4 oz) grated Parmesan cheese
55g (2 oz) dried breadcrumbs
2 tsp herbes de Provence
$^{1}/_{2}$ tsp Cayenne pepper
Salt and freshly ground black pepper

Wipe the chicken fillets with kitchen paper. Melt the butter. Mix all the dry ingredients together. Brush the chicken fillets with the melted butter, and then roll in the dry ingredients. Place the chicken on a piece of Bake-O-Glide on the cold plain shelf.

MAIN OVEN 220-230°C (425-450°F) GAS MARK 7-8
Place the shelf onto the floor of the oven and cook for 6-8 minutes. Turn the chicken fillets over to finish cooking and brown the other side.

SERVE WITH OVEN POTATO WEDGES
Wash the potatoes, complete with skins, and cut into wedges, toss in oil and place in a baking tray. Roast in a hot oven, turning occasionally.

TIP! Dry out breadcrumbs in a low oven.

COUSCOUS

An ideal accompaniment or served on its own as a salad. The fresh dates add a hint of sweetness.

SERVES 4
175g (6 oz) quick couscous
Chicken or vegetable stock, boiling
1 tbsp olive oil
1 tsp salt
Juice of 2 lemons
85g (3 oz) chopped parsley
55g (2 oz) pine nuts
1 red onion, finely chopped
4 tomatoes, chopped
6 fresh dates, stoned and chopped
Freshly ground black pepper

Make up the couscous according to the packet instructions. For a stock recipe and suggestions *see* p31. Place the couscous into a bowl and pour over the boiling stock. Add the oil and salt then leave to fluff up. Stir with a fork to separate.

Meanwhile prepare the other ingredients, then add them to the couscous and serve.

VARIATION
• Make up the couscous and mix with Roasted Mediterranean Vegetables, (*see* p76)

MELBA TOAST

This toast is ideal to serve with soups and pâtés.

Make the toast in the normal way by placing the bread directly on the hotplate, cook both sides. Remove all the crusts and cut down between the two toasted sides, so you have two very thin slices. Cut these into two and place for 2-4 minutes in a hot oven to curl.

CHEESE TORTILLA CRISPS Ⓥ

Timing on this quick snack recipe varies somewhat, dependent upon whether you like your tortillas chewy or crispy – the longer the cooking time the crisper they become.

PER PERSON
25-55g (1-2 oz) grated cheese
1 tortilla

Sprinkle the cheese over the tortilla and fold it in half. Place on the hotplate, at a simmering to moderate heat, for about 3-4 minutes to heat through. Using a metal spatula turn over and cook the other side.

Alternatively, the tortilla can be cooked on the floor of a hot Main Oven. Serve with a salsa (*see* p83), or salad.

VARIATION
• Add a slice of cooked ham to the cheese
• Sandwich together two tortillas and cut into wedges to serve.

MEXICAN TORTILLAS

MAKES 4
225g (8 oz) minced beef
1 small onion, finely chopped
1 chilli, deseeded and finely chopped
Salt and freshly ground black pepper
4 tortillas
To serve
Sour cream or crème fraîche
Guacamole

Turn up the cooker control and fry the minced beef on a high heat in a non-stick frying pan, add the onion, chilli and seasoning. Stir until the beef is cooked and browned.

Meanwhile, heat the tortillas in either the Main Oven or on the simmering side of the hotplate.

Assemble by dividing the meat mixture between the warmed tortillas, then add a blob of sour cream. Fold over or roll up into a 'wrap' and serve with the guacamole.

DEVILLED TOASTED SANDWICHES

Mix 115g (4 oz) of grated Lancashire cheese with 2 tbsp Worcestershire sauce and a shake of Tabasco, spread over slices of bread, top with slices of tomato and cover with another slice of bread. Toast both sides on the simmering side of the hotplate. Use slices of a French stick as an alternative.

Spread slices of bread with a little English mustard and cover with grated Cheshire cheese. Top with another slice of bread, and toast on the simmering side of the hotplate.

Crumble or grate 115g (4 oz) of Shropshire Blue cheese and mix with 25g (1 oz) of butter. Spread over slices of bread and cover with spicy mango chutney. Top with another slice of bread and toast on the simmering side of the hotplate.

OMELETTES Ⓥ

Use a 15cm (6 inch) omelette pan to make a classic three-egg omelette. A 23cm (9 inch) pan will require 4-5 eggs. The smaller size is perfect for one person.

SERVES 1
3 large free-range eggs
Pinch of salt
Freshly ground black pepper
Pinch of grated nutmeg
1 tbsp water
Knob of butter
Filling suggestions: choose one of the below
Sauté mushrooms
Grated cheese
Cooked chicken or ham
Goats' cheese and rocket

Using a fork, beat the eggs, salt, pepper, nutmeg and water, but not too thoroughly – you want some discernible strands of yolk and white.

Have your prepared filling and a serving plate ready. Both can be kept warm in the Lower Oven.

Heat the dry omelette pan on the hotplate for a good minute and then add the knob of butter. Swirl it around the pan, place back on the heat and wait until the butter is just starting to turn a light nutty brown. Add the eggs, and use the tines of the fork (pointing upwards) to gradually stir and fold the mixture.

When the mixture is three-quarters cooked, add your chosen filling. If you are adding a cold filling, such as cheese, sprinkle over and then transfer the pan to the very top of a hot oven for a couple of minutes. This will melt the cheese and finish cooking the omelette.

Alternatively, add any prepared hot filling and when the mixture is 'just cooked', turn deftly onto a warm plate, using two alternate folds to give the omelette a neat rolled-up presentation. Use a palette knife, if necessary, to help you.

Right
Mexican Tortillas

PIZZAS

QUICK BASE
Cheese scone mixture (*see* p126) – enough for 1 pizza

FAST BREAD BASE
One packet of white bread mix, made up – enough
for 2 pizzas

YEAST DOUGH BASE Ⓥ
10g (¹/₂ oz) fresh yeast
4 tbsp warm milk (not hot)
225g (8 oz) strong plain bread flour
1 tsp salt
1 egg
3-4 tbsp olive oil

Cream the yeast with the milk. Mix the flour with the
salt and place it by the Rayburn to warm. Add the
yeast mixture, egg and olive oil and mix well. Knead
until smooth. Place in a bowl and cover with cling film,
leave by the Rayburn until the dough is risen and light,
about 2 hours. Sprinkle the dough with flour and knock
back. Shape the dough into a circle or rectangle and
cover with the chosen topping.

BASIC TOMATO SAUCE Ⓥ
2 tbsp olive oil
1 onion, finely chopped
2 cloves of garlic, crushed
1 x 400g can of chopped tomatoes
1 tsp sugar
Salt and black pepper
1 tbsp tomato purée

Heat the olive oil in a pan on the hotplate, add the
onion and garlic and gently fry until soft. Add the
tomatoes, sugar, seasoning and the tomato purée
and cook until thickened to a spreading consistency.
Use this as a tomato base for spreading over the pizza
before adding the topping.

TOPPINGS

MARGHERITA
Sprinkle torn basil leaves over the tomato sauce and
place slices of Mozzarella on top.

CRAB AND ASPARAGUS
Spoon crabmeat and cooked asparagus over the
tomato sauce and sprinkle with grated Mozzarella.

HAWAIIAN
Place cubed fresh pineapple over the tomato sauce.
Sprinkle with diced, cooked ham or crispy bacon and
finally some grated cheese

MEXICAN
Spoon chilli con carne over the tomato sauce and
sprinkle with grated cheese.

ROASTED RED PEPPER,
SPINACH AND GOATS' CHEESE
Scatter roasted red peppers over the tomato sauce,
cover with a handful of spinach and arrange slices of
goat's cheese on top.

ROASTED VEGETABLE AND OLIVE
Spoon cooked roasted vegetables and sliced black
olives over the tomato sauce, cover with grated
cheese.

MAIN OVEN 220-230°C (425-450°F) GAS MARK 7-8
Place the pizza on a piece of Bake-O-Glide and in turn
place this on the floor of the oven. Bake for 8-15
minutes depending upon the pizza base and diameter.
Baking directly on the oven floor will ensure a crisp
base. If the base has cooked to your liking but the
cheese is not quite ready, move the pizza up to the
centre of the oven to finish baking.

BREAKFAST

Although most of us don't have a full cooked breakfast every day, when you do want to indulge in the full English classic, using the radiant heat from the Main Oven gives excellent results. Even eggs can be fried in a suitable container on the floor of the oven, up to nine at a time. Because the oven is vented, smells are minimised. The Lower Oven is perfect for keeping cooked food hot and warming plates. Cast-iron versions are excellent for slow cooking, making weekend breakfasts for large numbers easy. The hotplate can be used for quickly boiling kettles and for making delicious Rayburn toast.

AMERICAN MAPLE STACKS

MAKES 24
225g (8 oz) self raising flour
1 tsp baking powder
55g (2 oz) caster sugar
2 large eggs, beaten
300ml (¹/₂ pint) milk
To serve
Maple syrup

Loosen the lid of the maple syrup and place it on the top plate to warm. If the simmering end of your hotplate is a little on the hot side, raise the lid for a few minutes and allow it to cool while you make the batter. Sift the flour and baking powder into a bowl and add the sugar. Beat the eggs and add to the measured milk. Now mix all to a smooth batter and leave to stand for a few minutes.

HOTPLATE

Lightly oil the simmering end of the hotplate and spoon enough batter for one pancake onto the hotplate. Cook on both sides, turning when bubbles appear. Keep hot in a folded napkin. Serve the pancakes piled up with the syrup.

TIP! BREAKFAST PASTRIES

For the ultimate fresh continental breakfast, defrost some frozen unbaked croissants in the refrigerator overnight, covered with clingfilm. Make sure the tail sides are facing downwards. They will prove slowly, ready to cook in just seven minutes in a hot Main Oven the following morning. Alternatively, place some ready-to-cook pains au chocolat covered with clingfilm in the refrigerator overnight. They can then be baked in the same way.

TIP! MAGNIFICENT MUFFINS

Muffins make a great breakfast – *see* Muffin Factory pp124-126.

CINNAMON FRENCH TOAST

SERVES 4
4 slices of day-old bread
2 tbsp caster sugar
8 tbsp milk
1 large egg, beaten
A knob of butter
To serve
4 tbsp caster sugar
1 tsp ground cinnamon or *maple* or *golden syrup*

Using a sharp knife, remove the crusts from the bread. In a shallow bowl, add the sugar to the milk and place on the top plate until slightly warmed and the sugar has dissolved. Dip each slice on both sides into the milk and place on a plate. Add the egg to the remainder of the milk and mix well. In a non-stick pan, melt the butter over a moderate heat. Dip each slice in the egg and milk mixture and add to the pan. Move the pan to the simmering end of the hotplate if necessary. Alternatively, cook directly on a lightly buttered piece of Bake-O-Glide placed on the simmering end of the hotplate. When it has turned golden, turnover to cook the other side. Serve sprinkled with the spiced sugar or syrup which has been warmed in its container on the top plate with the lid loosened.

TOAST AND BAGELS

Slice the bread any thickness you like and place directly on the hotplate that must be at a medium to hot temperature – cook in the middle, or use the simmering end, depending on setting. With solid fuel models, toast may also be made using the heat from the fire if it is glowing brightly. Open the flue damper and ashpit spinwheel to give the best results, using a traditional toasting fork. For Melba toast, *see* p19).

Right
American Maple Stacks

LAZY OVEN BREAKFAST

Cooked breakfasts can be done to perfection with little mess using the Main Oven. Grill using a grill rack set in the high position at the top of the oven, or fry foods using a container on the floor of the oven.

PER PERSON
1 tomato
55g (2 oz) mushrooms
2 rashers of dry-cured bacon
1 good quality sausage
1 free-range egg
Salt and freshly ground black pepper

MAIN OVEN 200°C (400°F), GAS MARK 6 OR ABOVE

TO GRILL
Line a Rayburn meat tin with a piece of Bake-O-Glide. Halve the tomatoes and arrange with the mushrooms and season well. Place the sausages on a grill rack set in the high position above the tomatoes and mushrooms. Slide the tin onto the top set of runners to grill the sausages and bake the items below. No extra fat will be needed. Once browned, turn the sausages. When evenly cooked, move the sausages down to sit next to the tomatoes and mushrooms, and add the bacon to the grill rack. Return to the very top of the oven and cook to your taste.

TO FRY
Place all the ingredients except the eggs in a Rayburn meat tin and cook with the tin on the oven floor.
If cooking for just one or two, use a cast-iron frying pan or baking dish. For very crisp bacon, cook this in a container on the floor of the oven. When everything is almost ready, remove items to keep warm on plates in the Lower Oven. Crack the eggs into the base of the tin or cast-iron pan. Cook on the floor of the oven to fry the eggs to taste. Alternatively fry, poach or scramble the eggs in a pre-heated pan on the hotplate. For fat-free fried eggs, cook on a piece of Bake-O-Glide on the simmering end of the hotplate. Adding a few drops of water around the eggs and covering with a Pyrex frying pan lid will create steam to speed up the cooking.

VARIATIONS
Add a slice of black pudding, a small, diced cooked potato, a slice of bread brushed with oil, or a kidney, skinned and sliced. Cook in the meat tin with the other ingredients.

GRANOLA CEREAL

MAKES 10-12 SERVINGS
450g (1 lb) rolled oats
55g (2 oz) wheatgerm
55g (2 oz) desiccated coconut
55g (2 oz) sunflower or sesame seeds
55g (2 oz) chopped blanched almonds
55g (2 oz) quartered blanched hazelnuts
90ml (3 fl oz) sunflower oil
50ml (2 fl oz) clear honey or maple syrup
1 tsp vanilla extract
55g (2 oz) dried banana chips
115g (4 oz) ready-to-eat raisins

Mix the first six ingredients together in a large bowl. Warm the oil and honey in a pan and stir in the vanilla. Add to the bowl and mix thoroughly. Spread out in a thin layer on baking trays.

MAIN OVEN 120°C (250°F), GAS MARK L-1
🅒 LOWER OVEN IN SLOW COOKING MODE
Bake in a slow oven until dried out. Stir every 30 minutes until a light golden colour, then leave to finish drying out on a chef's pad on top of the closed insulated lids overnight. When perfectly dried, cool, and then mix in the banana and raisins. Store in an airtight container for up to a month.

OVEN KIPPERS

PER PERSON
1 un-dyed smoked kipper
A knob of unsalted butter
Freshly ground black pepper
1/4 of a fresh lemon

MAIN OVEN 200°C (400°F), GAS MARK 6
Grill or poach the kippers in the Main Oven. To grill, dot with butter, place on a grill rack and cook on the top set of runners for 10-15 minutes. Alternatively, place in shallow container with just enough boiling water to cover, cook for 5-10 minutes near the top of the Main Oven until just cooked. Season with the pepper and serve with the lemon wedge.

Right
Lazy Oven Breakfast

OVERNIGHT YOGHURT

MAKES 1 LITRE
1 litre carton of UHT milk
2 tbsp dried skimmed milk powder
2 tbsp live natural yoghurt

MAIN OVEN 120°C (250°F), GAS MARK L-1
Place the milk carton on the coolest part of the top plate of the Rayburn for 15-30 minutes, and warm to 'blood heat' – approx. 37°C (98°F). Pour the warm milk into a bowl or 1 litre Pyrex jug. Whisk in the dried milk powder and then stir in the live yoghurt. Cover with a plate or clingfilm and place on a chef's pad or folded cloth on a closed insulated lid at the coolest end of the hotplate. Leave the mixture undisturbed for 10 hours, overnight is ideal. Once set, chill before serving.

POACHED FRUIT COMPOTE

115g (4 oz) dried mixed fruit compôte
600ml (1 pint) cold Earl Grey tea
300ml (¹/₂ pint) clear apple juice
1 tbsp runny honey

MAIN OVEN 120°C (250°F), GAS MARK L-1
Ⓒ LOWER OVEN IN SLOW COOKING MODE
Place all the ingredients in a pan with a tight-fitting lid. Bring almost to the boil and then cover and transfer low down in the Main Oven until the fruit is plump and tender – at least 30 minutes.

VARIATION
Use a breakfast tea and add a cinnamon stick.

RAYBURN PORRIDGE

SERVES 4
For an authentic overnight Rayburn porridge, use medium pinhead oatmeal, obtainable from health food shops. For fast porridge made with rolled oats, use the top plate method.

OVERNIGHT PORRIDGE
600ml (1 pint) water
A pinch of salt
75g (3 oz) medium pinhead oatmeal

For overnight porridge: measure the water into a heavy-based pan that has a well-fitting lid. Last thing at night, bring to the boil with the salt and pour in the oatmeal, stirring well. Transfer the pan to the simmering end of the hotplate and cook for 5 minutes, stirring occasionally.

MAIN OVEN 120°C (250°F), GAS MARK L-1
Cover and transfer to a grid shelf on the floor of the oven.

FAST PORRIDGE
2 cups water
A pinch of salt
1 cup rolled oats
Milk to serve

For fast porridge: mix the water with the rolled oats in a pan last thing at night. With the cooker at an idling setting, leave the pan tightly covered on the top plate to gently cook overnight. In the morning, bring to a simmer on the hotplate, and add enough milk to obtain your preferred consistency.

SODA BREAD FARLS

White, wholemeal or a mixture of flours may be used, using half and half is recommended, and up to 55g (2 oz) of fine oatmeal can also be substituted, if preferred.

MAKES 4 LARGE FARLS
450g (1 lb) plain flour
1 tsp bicarbonate of soda
1 tsp salt
Approx. 400ml (14 fl oz) buttermilk

Sieve the flour with the bicarbonate of soda then add the bran from the sieve with the oatmeal, if using, and then add the salt. Make a well in the centre and add most of the milk. Working quickly, mix to a soft, not too sticky consistency. When it coheres into a ball, turn it onto a well-floured surface and lightly work into a flattened loaf. Place on a rectangle of Bake-O-Glide lightly dusted with flour, and use a sharp knife to cut a deep cross in the top.

MAIN OVEN 200°C (400°F), GAS MARK 6
Bake on the floor of the Main Oven for 30-40 minutes. To test if it is cooked, tap the underside, it should sound hollow. Serve while still warm with soup and cheese, or with butter and jam. When day-old, toast before serving.

VARIATIONS

SWEET

Add the following to the basic recipe:
1 tbsp caster sugar
$\frac{1}{2}$ tsp mixed spice
115g (4 oz) sultanas
Grated zest of a lemon

SAVOURY

Add one of the following to the basic recipe:
115g (4 oz) black olives
or 115g (4 oz) caramelised onions
or 115g (4 oz) sun-blushed tomatoes

SOUPS AND STARTERS

There are many different types of soup and we have included recipes for both light soups that make good appetisers, as well as the more robust soups that are ideal as a lunchtime meal. Depending on the recipe, soup can either be cooked on the hotplate, or cooked slowly in the oven.

The starter recipes include those that are traditionally served as a first course, such as Easy Chicken Liver Pâté (p35), and those to be served less formally, such as canapés. The Bruschetta and Crostini (both also p35) make wonderful canapés. They are toasted and grilled in the Main Oven and create a real 'wow' factor when they emerge.

STOCK

Stock is well worth the small amount of time it takes to prepare. Soups, casseroles and gravies gain more flavour if you add homemade stock, even packet soups can be up-lifted by adding some. The Rayburn is ideal for making stock, especially if you use the low heat of the Main Oven, or the cast-iron Lower Oven when the Main Oven is hot.

If you make large quantities, any excess can be frozen to use at a later date. The best way to freeze any extra is in a small square container or freezer bag. Also worth trying is to reduce the stock to a more concentrated state and then freeze it in ice-cube trays.

BASIC STOCK
The proportions can be varied; a rule of thumb is 450g (1 lb) solid ingredients to 2 litres (3½ pints) of water, which makes about 1.2 litres (2 pints) finished stock.

450g (1 lb) bones – meat, poultry or fish
2 litres (3½ pints) cold water
1 tsp salt
6 peppercorns
2 large carrots, cleaned and cut into large pieces
1 large onion, peeled and chopped
1 stick of celery, washed and cut into large pieces
1 bay leaf
Parsley stems (tops and stalks)

Place the bones into a heavy-based saucepan with a well fitting lid and metal handle. Pour over the water and add the salt and crushed peppercorns. Bring slowly to the boil, removing any scum. Add the carrots, onion, celery, bay leaf and parsley and bring back to the boil.

MAIN OVEN 150°C (300°F) GAS MARK 2
Transfer the stock to the oven to simmer for 3 hours (for fish stock, 45 minutes is plenty).

Strain the stock, taste, and if necessary boil rapidly to concentrate the flavour. Taste once more and then pour into a basin. Cool, place in the fridge. Skim off any fat that has risen to the top of the stock. At this point it can be used or frozen.

TIP! If short of time then use the following for flavourings
• Good quality stock cube or powder.
• Yeast-extract, such as Marmite.
• Substitute an appropriate colour wine for a quarter of the liquid required.

CROUTONS ⓥ

Remove the crusts from 4 slices of thick-sliced white bread; the bread is better for being a day or two old. Cut the bread into cubes. Melt 25g (1 oz) of butter with 2 tbsp of olive oil and gently fry on the hotplate, turning regularly until the cubes are crisp and golden brown. Alternatively, if the Main Oven is at moderate, cook off in the Rayburn meat tin, again turning or shaking regularly.

VARIATIONS
• For garlic flavoured croûtons; crush one clove of garlic into the butter and oil.
• Use a chilli-flavoured oil for croûtons with a zing.
• Use truffle-flavoured oil for croûtons to accompany mushroom soup.

BROCCOLI AND STILTON SOUP

SERVES 8
25g (1 oz) butter
1 tbsp oil
1 large onion, finely chopped
1 clove of garlic, crushed (optional)
450g (1 lb) broccoli
1 large potato, peeled and diced
1.2litre (2 pint) stock (chicken, or use Marigold bouillon powder)
225g (8 oz) Blue Stilton
600ml (1 pint) milk
150ml (5 fl oz) double cream
Salt and freshly ground black pepper
Freshly grated nutmeg

On the simmering side of the hotplate melt the butter and oil in a large heavy-based pan. Add the onion and stir for a couple of minutes. Add the garlic if using, cover and move the pan so that it is only just on the hotplate. This will allow the onion to cook slowly until tender.

Cut off the broccoli florets and put to one side. Chop the stalks into roughly 2.5cm (1 inch) pieces. Add the potato to the pan and cook on the simmering end of the hotplate until well coated with the butter. Add the stalks and stock, transfer to the boiling end of the hotplate and bring to a boil. Adjust the pan on the hotplate to gently simmer until the stalks are tender. Add the florets and cook for a further 3-5 minutes at a full boil until just tender, but retaining a vibrant green colour.

Take off the heat and liquidise in batches with the Stilton. Return to the rinsed pan and add the milk. Heat until piping hot, then add the cream and adjust the seasoning to taste. Serve with warm crusty bread.

FRENCH ONION SOUP

SERVES 4-6
55g (2 oz) butter
700g (1¹/₂ lb) onions, quartered and sliced
3 cloves of garlic, crushed
1-2 tsp sugar
Salt and black pepper
300ml (¹/₂ pint) white wine
600ml (1 pint) stock
2 tsp Worcestershire sauce
Topping
8 slices of Baguettine (narrow French bread)
25g (1 oz) Gruyère cheese, grated
Garnish
Chopped chives

Melt the butter in a large pan. Add the onions, garlic and sugar. Cover the pan and gently cook the onions until soft, but not coloured, this should take about 10-15 minutes. Alternatively, soften the onions in a low oven for about 20 minutes; this means that cooking smells will be reduced in the kitchen.

Remove the lid from the pan and cook until the liquid has reduced and the onions are just beginning to brown. Season and add the wine, stock and Worcestershire sauce. Bring to the boil.

HOTPLATE
Simmer on the hotplate for about 1 hour.

MAIN OVEN 120°C (250°F) GAS MARK L-1
Ⓒ **LOWER OVEN IN SLOW COOKING MODE**
Simmer for 5 minutes then transfer to the oven for 1 hour.

Meanwhile make the topping. Place the slices of bread onto a piece of Bake-O-Glide on the plain shelf and divide the Gruyère cheese between them. Place the shelf directly on the floor of a hot oven and cook for about 5 minutes, until the bases are browned and the cheese is beginning to melt on top.

To serve Place the slices of cheese toast into a tureen or bowl and ladle over the soup. Each person should have a slice of cheese toast with their soup. Bon appetite!

HARICOT BEAN SOUP

If you don't have any ham stock, add a ham-hock to the ingredients and use water instead. It will turn into stock within the soup as it gently cooks.

SERVES 8
350g (12 oz) haricot beans
1 large onion, roughly chopped
1 clove garlic, crushed
1.7 litre (3 pints) ham stock
25g (1 oz) butter
Salt and freshly ground white pepper
A little milk, if required
2-3 tbsp cream (optional)
1 tbsp chopped fresh parsley

Soak the beans in cold water and leave overnight in a cool place. Drain and rinse the beans in a colander. Add to a large pan with the onion, garlic and stock. Bring to the boil on the boiling end of the hotplate, then move to the other end of the hotplate and simmer for 5 minutes.

MAIN OVEN 120°C (250°F), GAS MARK L-1
Ⓒ **LOWER OVEN IN SLOW COOKING MODE**
Cover and then transfer to the floor of the oven for 2 hours. The beans should become very soft. Allow to cool a little and then liquidise in batches. For the silkiest finish, pass through a fine sieve to remove the skins, or leave them in if you prefer. Lastly, whisk in the butter and adjust the seasoning. If the soup seems a little thick, slacken down with some milk or further stock. A little cream may be added, then sprinkle over the parsley. Serve piping hot.

JERUSALEM ARTICHOKE AND CARROT SOUP

The addition of carrots makes this a delicately coloured soup. Jerusalem artichokes are very easy to grow in your own garden. The tubers are in season all through winter.

SERVES 6-8
550g (1¼ lb) Jerusalem artichokes, peeled
1 litre (2 pints) chicken stock or water
Juice of 1 lemon
225g (8 oz) carrots, peeled and cut into pieces
1 medium onion, chopped
1 tsp salt
Freshly ground black pepper
4 tbsp single cream
Garnish
2 tbsp chopped fresh parsley

Place the artichokes into the stock, or water, and add the lemon juice. Tip in the carrots and onion, then season. Bring to the boil.

HOTPLATE
Simmer on the hotplate for 30-40 minutes.
MAIN OVEN 120°C (250°F) GAS MARK L-1
Ⓖ LOWER OVEN IN SLOW COOKING MODE
Simmer for 5 minutes then transfer to the oven for 30-40 minutes.

Remove from the oven or hotplate and liquidise the soup until smooth. Add the cream and reheat. Serve sprinkled with chopped fresh parsley.

SHROPSHIRE PEA SOUP WITH A HINT OF MINT Ⓥ

SERVES 6-8
55g (2 oz) butter
1 onion, finely chopped
700g (1½ lb) fresh peas, shelled
1 litre (1¾ pint) stock
Salt and freshly ground black pepper
¼ tsp sugar
2 sprigs mint
150ml (¼ pint) double cream
Garnish
115g (4 oz) cooked peas
1 tbsp chopped fresh mint

Heat the butter in a saucepan, add the onion and cook until soft. Add the peas and cook over a low heat until the butter has been absorbed. Stir in the stock and season to taste. Add the sugar and mint sprigs.

HOTPLATE
Simmer for 10 minutes, or until the peas are tender.

Purée the soup and add the cream. Reheat the soup but do not boil. Check the seasoning and serve garnished with the cooked whole peas and chopped mint.

TOMATO AND LENTIL SOUP Ⓥ

SERVES 4
115g (4 oz) red lentils
850ml (1½ pints) stock
1 onion, peeled and chopped
1 x 400g can of chopped tomatoes
2 tsp fresh thyme
Salt and freshly ground black pepper
Garnish
Chopped fresh parsley
Croûtons

Place all the ingredients into a saucepan and bring to the boil on the hotplate.

HOTPLATE
Simmer on the hotplate for about 45-60 minutes.

MAIN OVEN 120°C (250°F) GAS MARK L-1
Ⓒ **LOWER OVEN**
Simmer for 5 minutes then transfer to the oven for about 1 hour.

Once cooked, you may liquidise if preferred. Adjust the seasoning and garnish with the chopped fresh parsley and croûtons.

THAI FISH AND COCONUT SOUP

SERVES 4-6
350g (12 oz) smoked haddock
2 tsp Thai fish sauce
1 tbsp oil
1 red chilli, finely chopped
1 green chilli, finely chopped
6 spring onions, sliced
115g (4 oz) baby corn, finely sliced
850ml (1¹/₂ pints) light stock
1 x 200ml carton coconut milk
2 tbsp lime juice
1 tbsp Thai fish sauce
Garnish
Chopped fresh coriander

Cut the fish into 1cm (¹/₂ inch) cubes and sprinkle with the Thai fish sauce.

HOTPLATE
Heat the oil in a large saucepan and fry the chilli, onions and baby corn for a minute. Pour over the stock and the coconut milk and bring to the boil. Simmer for 5 minutes. Add the fish and cook for a further 2-4 minutes until the fish is cooked.

Add the lime juice and the fish sauce, taste and adjust the seasoning. Serve garnished with the chopped fresh coriander.

TUSCAN BEAN SOUP

SERVES 8
350g (12 oz) mixed dried beans, rinsed, such as black-eyed, haricot, kidney, pinto or soya, etc.
1 tbsp olive oil
1 large onion, chopped
1 small leek, finely sliced
4 cloves of garlic, crushed
600ml (1 pint) vegetable stock
900ml (1¹/₂ pints) water
1 x 400g can of chopped tomatoes
115g (4 oz) frozen peas
1 tbsp green pesto
Salt and freshly ground black pepper
4 tbsp chopped fresh parsley

Soak the beans in cold water overnight in a cool place. Drain and rinse the beans in a colander. Add to a large pan and cover with 5cm (2 inches) cold water. Bring to the boil on the boiling end of the hotplate, then move to the other end of the hotplate and simmer for 5 minutes.

MAIN OVEN 120°C (250°F) GAS MARK L-1
Ⓒ **LOWER OVEN IN SLOW COOKING MODE**
Cover and then transfer to the floor of the oven for about an hour. The beans should cook until they are tender. Drain in a colander, discarding the cooking liquid.

Increase the setting of the cooker and heat the oil in the rinsed pan. Add the onion, leek and garlic and cook gently until soft but not coloured. Add the stock, water and bring to the boil. Add the cooked beans and simmer on the simmering end of the hotplate for 10 minutes. Add the tomatoes and simmer for a further 10-15 minutes. Return the pan to the boiling end of the hotplate and add the peas and pesto. Cook for 3 minutes, and then remove from the heat.

Allow to cool a little and then purée a quarter of the soup. Taste to adjust the seasoning, bring back to just a simmer and add the parsley just before serving. This recipe can be made a day ahead and, if anything, is even better on re-heating.

TIP! A mixture of drained canned beans may be used instead.

BRUSCHETTA Ⓥ

From the Italian meaning 'to roast over coals', bruschetta are traditional garlic bread. They can be cooked on the floor of a hot Main Oven, or can be 'grilled' using a cast-iron grill pan. Place slices of ciabatta brushed with olive oil into a hot grill pan and cook until 'branded' with stripes on both sides. Rub the bread with a garlic clove and season with sea salt and black pepper. Serve warm.

VARIATIONS
- Serve topped with chopped ripe tomatoes and torn basil leaves.
- Top with tomato and Mozzarella slices.
- Top with crumbled Gorgonzola cheese mixed with a little Mascarpone and garnished with a walnut half.

CROSTINI Ⓥ

Literally, this is Italian for 'little toasts'. They consist of toasted bread with various savoury toppings.

Cut a small narrow loaf such as a baguette into slices, about 1 cm ($\frac{1}{2}$ inch) thick. Spread with a garlic soft cheese, such as Boursin and top with a slice of tomato and some sliced olives. Sprinkle with grated cheese and place on a piece of Bake-O-Glide on a baking tray. Place direct on the floor of the Main Oven at 200°C (400°F) Gas Mark 6 to toast and grill for about 8-10 minutes. Serve garnished with watercress.

VARIATIONS
- Spread with a little pesto in place of the Boursin.
- Top with tomato slice, season and cover with goats' cheese.
- Brush the bread both sides with olive oil, toast uncovered, serve spread with tapenade topped with Parma ham and a basil leaf.

EASY CHICKEN LIVER PATE

This is a quick recipe, which has proved popular time and time again.

SERVES 4-6
25g (1 oz) butter
1 onion, finely chopped
1 clove of garlic, finely chopped
350g (12 oz) chicken livers, cleaned, cored and roughly chopped
1 tbsp cream
2 tbsp brandy
Salt and freshly ground black pepper
Knob of butter
115g (4 oz) button mushrooms, sliced
55g (2 oz) butter, melted

Melt the butter and sauté the onion and garlic until transparent. Add the chicken livers and cook for 10 minutes until cooked through. Remove from the heat and place in a processor or liquidiser, add the cream and brandy. Season. Process to make a smooth paste.

Melt the knob of butter and sauté the mushrooms until just cooked, about 2-3 minutes. Stir the mushrooms into the chicken liver mixture and turn into a dish. Pour over the cooled melted butter and refrigerate. Serve with toast and a tomato and orange chutney, or similar.

MUSSEL FACTORY
MOULES MARINIERE

SERVES 4
1.8 kg (4 pints or 4 lb) mussels
25g (1 oz) butter
1 small onion, finely chopped
2 cloves garlic, crushed
150ml ($\frac{1}{4}$ pint) dry white wine
4 tbsp double cream (optional)
Salt and freshly ground black pepper
2 tbsp chopped fresh parsley

Melt the butter in a large pan and gently soften the onion and garlic on the simmering end of the hotplate. Add the wine and as soon as it comes to the boil, add the prepared mussels. Cover with a lid and place on the boiling end of the hotplate for 5 minutes.

Remove from the heat and lift out the mussels using a slotted spoon and keep warm. Discard any mussels that have not opened up and any empty half-shells. Pass the cooking liquid through a sieve lined with muslin to remove the onion, garlic and any grit from the mussels and discard.

Return the liquid to the pan and boil hard until reduced by half. With the pan on the simmering end of the hotplate, add the cream, if using. Season lightly and add the parsley. Divide the mussels between warmed serving soup plates and pour over the sauce. Serve with crusty bread.

TIP! To prepare mussels, check that they are all tightly shut before using. If any are open, tap smartly on the work surface; if they do not close within a few seconds, they are dead and should be discarded, together with any with broken shells. Scrape off any barnacles and wash the mussels well in several changes of cold water, removing any beards that are attached.

PROVENCALE

Increase the garlic to 4 cloves, omit the cream and add 1 x 400g can of drained chopped plum tomatoes with 1 tsp of sugar and 2 tbsp of chopped fresh basil (or 2 tsp of dried oregano).

NORMANDY

Replace the wine with cider and add thin slices of a peeled dessert apple with the cream. Add a dash of Calvados just before serving.

KORMA

Use a light chicken or vegetable stock in place of the wine. Add to the onion and garlic, a 1cm ($\frac{1}{2}$ inch) piece of sliced ginger, three lightly crushed cardamom pods and a generous pinch of saffron. Stir 1 tbsp of cornflour into 150ml (5 fl oz) of natural yoghurt and add with the cream. Heat through over a low heat until just bubbling and simmer gently for 3 minutes before serving.

THAI

Add 1-2 red chillies, finely chopped and 1 stalk of lemon grass, beaten flat and cut into three pieces with the onion and garlic. Omit the cream and add 2 tbsp of fish sauce (nam pla) and 2-3 tbsp of chopped fresh coriander before serving.

PESTO AND SMOKED SALMON DROP SCONES

MAKES 20
115g (4 oz) self raising flour
1 egg
2 tbsp Pesto sauce
100ml (4 fl oz) milk
Salt and freshly ground black pepper
Olive oil
Topping
Crème fraîche or *sour cream*
55g (2oz) smoked salmon, make up into small rolls
Garnish
Lemon wedges
Chopped fresh parsley or *dill*

Place the flour in a basin and make a well in the centre. Add the egg, pesto sauce and half the milk, whisk together and thin to a dropping consistency with the remaining milk. Season.

Wipe the simmering end of the hotplate with a little oil on a piece of kitchen paper. Drop tablespoons of the mixture onto the hotplate, when bubbles rise to the surface, turn over and cook the other side. Leave to cool in a clean tea-towel.

Place the pancakes on a serving plate, top each pancake with a spoon of sour cream and a roll of smoked salmon. Garnish with the lemon and chopped parsley or dill.

Right
Pesto and Smoked Salmon Drop Scones

ROASTED ASPARAGUS SPEARS (v)

This is ideal for thicker English green asparagus, in season during May and June.

SERVES 4
12 asparagus spears
2 tbsp olive oil
Sea salt
Garnish
Shavings of Parmesan cheese
Balsamic vinegar
4 soft boiled quails' eggs (optional)

Prepare the asparagus by snapping off the tough, woody lower parts of the stems. Each spear should be about the same length. Place them on a shallow baking tray, lined with Bake-O-Glide. Brush the spears with the olive oil and sprinkle with the salt.

MAIN OVEN 220°C (425°F) GAS MARK 7
Roast at the top of the oven (turning over once), for 10-15 minutes, until tender.

Serve on warmed plates, garnished with shavings of Parmesan, and sprinkle with drops of good Balsamic vinegar. Place two halves of a quail's egg on the side of the plate, if using.

SEARED SCALLOPS AND MIXED LEAF SALAD

SERVES 4
8 prepared scallops
2 tbsp oil
15g (^{1}/$_2$ oz) butter
Juice of half a lemon
Mixed salad leaves
Balsamic vinaigrette

If the scallops are large, slice in two. Heat a heavy based pan on the hottest side of the hotplate, then add the oil, swirl around for a few seconds and lay the scallops in the pan.

Cook for about ^{1}/$_2$-1 minute until beginning to turn brown underneath. Turn over using a palette knife and cook for a further ^{1}/$_2$-1 minute. Add the butter and lemon juice, swirl around and tip the scallops and liquor into a bowl of mixed salad leaves. Quickly dress with the vinaigrette and mix together. Serve at once.

SMOKED HADDOCK APPETISERS

These can be made up in advance and kept in the refrigerator. If you do refrigerate, allow a little extra cooking time to ensure they are heated right through.

SERVES 6
225g (8 oz) smoked haddock
250ml (^{1}/$_2$ pint) milk
Freshly ground black pepper
1 bay leaf
25g (1 oz) butter
25g (1 oz) plain flour
115g (4 oz) prawns
225g (8 oz) cooked mashed potato
1 egg yolk
Pinch freshly ground nutmeg
Garnish
6 prawns in their shells
Dill

Place the haddock into an ovenproof dish and cover with the milk, season with the pepper and tuck in a bay leaf.

MAIN OVEN 220°C (425°F) GAS MARK 7
Cook in the centre of the oven for about 15 minutes, until the fish is just cooked.

Remove the skin from the fish and discard, separate the fish into large flakes. Strain the milk and place into a saucepan with the butter and flour. Place the pan on the Simmering Plate and whisk the milk continuously until the sauce comes to the boil and thickens. Add the fish flakes and the prawns and divide the mixture between 6 ramekin dishes.

Right
Roasted Asparagus Spears

Place the mashed potato into a basin and mix in the egg yolk and nutmeg, place in a piping bag and pipe the potato over the fish mixture. Alternatively, just pile the potato mixture on and fluff up with a fork.

Place the ramekins onto a baking tray and slide onto the grid shelf on the second set of runners. Cook for about 15 minutes, until browned.

Serve piping hot, garnished with a prawn and a sprig of dill.

VARIATION
• Add chopped dill or parsley to the sauce.

SPINACH ROULADE Ⓥ

A lovely tasty starter, or light main course. Use fresh spinach for the best flavour.

SERVES 6-8
450g (1 lb) fresh spinach
Pinch of grated nutmeg
25g (1 oz) freshly grated Parmesan cheese
Salt and freshly gound black pepper
4 eggs, separated
Filling
25g (1 oz) butter
1 clove of garlic, crushed
115g (4 oz) mushrooms, sliced
25g (1 oz) plain flour
200ml (7 fl oz) milk
Salt and freshly ground black pepper

Wash the spinach leaves, cook with just the water left clinging to the leaves. Drain very well and then chop. Place in a basin with the nutmeg, Parmesan and season. Mix well. Add the egg yolks. Whisk the egg whites until stiff and fold into the spinach mixture. Pour into a greased and lined Swiss-roll tin measuring 28cm x 18cm (11 x 7 inch).

MAIN OVEN 180°C (350°F) GAS MARK 4
Cook in the centre of the oven for about 15 minutes or until firm.

Meanwhile, make the filling sauce by melting the butter. Gently sauté the garlic and mushrooms in the butter, then add the flour, gradually add the milk. Bring to the boil, stirring until thickened. Place in the Lower Oven until ready to use.

Invert the cooked roulade onto a sheet of Bake-O-Glide and carefully remove the lining paper. Spread the sauce over the roulade and roll up firmly. Serve in slices warm or cold.

VARIATION
• For a Spinach and Prawn Roulade omit the mushrooms and use 225g (8 oz) of cooked prawns and 2 tbsp of chopped fresh parsley added to the sauce at the final stage.

MEAT, POULTRY AND GAME

Due to the indirect heat of the cast-iron Rayburn oven, roasts are easy to cook to perfection. As well as traditional fast roasting, slow roasts and one-pot dishes are also a special forte of the Rayburn. The most wonderful casseroles can be cooked when your oven is at an idling setting, off-peak between meals, or overnight.

FRYING

For frying meat or poultry on the hotplate, a high temperature is required and the cooker should be turned up to a high setting. Oven-frying is also possible using the floor of a hot Main Oven, and this technique minimises mess on the top of the cooker.

GRILLING

There are two ways of grilling meat on a Rayburn; use the special cast-iron grill pan to grill steaks, chops and cutlets on the hotplate using the same principle as a charcoal grill. With the cooker at a high setting, pre-heat a clean and dry cast-iron grill pan on the simmering end of the hotplate before transferring to the boiling end for 3-4 minutes to absorb the full amount of heat ready for cooking. Brush the ridges with a little fat taken from the side of the meat and then add the meat.

Alternatively, lightly oil the food (but never the pan). Press the meat down lightly so it makes good contact and cook for 1-2 minutes a side for rare, or if you prefer, a minute longer each side. Once the meat has been added to the pan, you can transfer the pan to finish cooking in the top of the Main Oven. Splashes and smells will then be taken away to the outside. The pan can also be pre-heated in the Main Oven beforehand, if preferred.

For other meats; grill by placing the food on a grill rack, placed in the high position in the meat tin and hang at the top of a hot Main Oven on the highest set of runners. Sausages and bacon cook beautifully here (see 'Breakfast' chapter, page 26), as do burgers, meat patties and thick pork chops.

ROASTING

When roasting meat, the radiant heat from the cast-iron oven seals in all the juices, ensuring amazingly moist roasts and wonderful crackling. The all round heat means exceptionally even cooking so you virtually never have to baste a joint. Shrinkage will be minimal, and the results moist and flavoursome. Only a little smearing of extra fat is needed for the leanest joints. Season to taste before roasting. Remember that if a joint is stuffed, weigh after it has been stuffed to calculate the correct cooking times.

There are two main methods of roasting in the Rayburn. The Fast Method is the best for the tenderest and better cuts of meat. The Slow Method is better for coarser cuts of meat, the long slow cooking rendering them meltingly tender with a great flavour. With models featuring a cast-iron Lower Oven, a further slow method is possible, when the Main Oven is at 200°C (400°F), Gas Mark 6 or above.

FAST ROASTING METHOD
(Main Oven, all models)
MAIN OVEN 200°C (400°F), GAS MARK 6

Season the meat and place in the Rayburn meat tin. Stand on the grill rack set in the low position if preferred. The use of a meat thermometer is recommended. It is then possible to ensure that meat and poultry are safely roasted and the two extremes of under and over cooking are avoided. (If you add a few onions and root vegetables with the meat, they will roast and brown, ensuring a rich and flavoursome gravy.) Hang the tin on the fourth set of runners in the Main Oven for the calculated time. (See the Roasting Matrix, opposite, for a guide to calculate cooking times.) When the meat is cooked, allow the joint to rest in the Lower Oven or next to the cooker for 15-30 minutes before carving.

SLOW ROASTING METHOD
(Main Oven, all models)
MAIN OVEN 180°C (350°F), GAS MARK 4

Season the meat and place in the Rayburn meat tin and prepare as for Fast Roasting. Hang the tin on the fourth set of runners in the Main Oven and roast for the calculated time. Turn the oven to a higher setting, 30 minutes before the expected finishing time. The oven will then begin to rise in temperature, ready for being quickly brought to a high setting to finish cooking any roast vegetables and trimmings.

VERY SLOW ROASTING METHOD
(cast-iron Lower Ovens only)
MAIN OVEN 200°C (400°F), GAS MARK 6

Season and prepare the meat as for other roasting methods. Calculate the total cooking time as for Fast Roasting. Hang the tin on the fourth set of runners in the Main Oven and allow 30 minutes for the roast to start cooking and begin to brown. (However, allow 45 minutes for roasts weighing more than 3.6kg (8 lbs).) Then transfer to continue to slow roast in the cast-iron Lower Oven for double the remaining cooking time. Return to the Main Oven at the end of the cooking to crisp if necessary, before the final resting. *For example, a 1.8kg (4 lb) leg of lamb, medium-roasted will require 20 minutes per 450g (1 lb) plus 20 minutes, so this gives a total time of 100 minutes. Begin in the Main Oven for 30 minutes and then transfer for double the remaining cooking time in the cast-iron Lower Oven, which is 140 minutes (2 hours and 20 minutes).*

MEAT ROASTING MATRIX

	FAST ROASTING Main Oven 200°C (400°F), Gas Mark 6	SLOW ROASTING Main Oven 180°C (350°F), Gas Mark 4
BEEF Rare Medium Well done	12 minutes per 450g (1 lb) + 12 minutes 15 minutes per 450g (1 lb) + 15 minutes 20 minutes per 450g (1 lb) + 20 minutes	20 minutes per 450g (1 lb) + 20 minutes 25 minutes per 450g (1 lb) + 25 minutes 30 minutes per 450g (1 lb) + 30 minutes
Fillet	10 minutes per 450g (1 lb) + 10 minutes	not suitable
LAMB Pink Medium	15 minutes per 450g (1 lb) + 15 minutes 20 minutes per 450g (1 lb) + 20 minutes	30 minutes per 450g (1 lb) + 30 minutes 35 minutes per 450g (1 lb) + 35 minutes
PORK	30 minutes per 450g (1 lb) + 30 minutes	35 minutes per 450g (1 lb) + 35 minutes
VEAL	20 minutes per 450g (1 lb) + 20 minutes	30 minutes per 450g (1 lb) + 30 minutes

Note: all cooking times are approximate

POT ROASTING AND DUTCH OVENS
MAIN OVEN 150°C (300°F), GAS MARK 2

Pot roasts should be cooked in a casserole in the Main Oven at a low temperature, over a long period of time. This way they become delicious and tender. Dutch ovens are mainly designed for slow roasting joints, covered, on the top of a cooker over a low heat source. Once started on the hotplate at the hotter end, these can also be transferred to the Main Oven at an idling setting and will cook meat to perfection.

POULTRY AND GAME

Roast poultry and game develops a wonderfully crisp skin on the outside giving way to deliciously moist tender flesh underneath. Most poultry is best cooked in the Main Oven by the Fast Method. A large turkey can alternatively be cooled slowly over many hours or overnight using the Slow Method; this is not recommended for smaller turkeys as they become cooked too quickly. It is important that all boned and rolled turkey joints are only cooked using the Fast Method (the Slow Method is not suitable for these roasts and should not be used). The use of a meat and poultry thermometer is strongly recommended. With models featuring a cast-iron Lower Oven, a further very slow method is possible for chicken only, when the Main Oven is at 200°C (400°F), Gas Mark 6 or above.

FAST ROASTING METHOD
(Main Oven, all models)
MAIN OVEN 200°C (400°F), GAS MARK 6

Season the poultry and place in the Rayburn meat tin or stand on the grill rack if preferred. Stuff the cavity of the bird with onion, lemon or herbs and smear the breast with a little softened butter; lastly, cover with some streaky bacon. Hang the tin on the fourth set of runners in the Main Oven for the calculated time, basting occasionally, although this is not as important as with conventional cookers. To check that the bird is thoroughly cooked, pierce the thickest part of the thigh with a skewer and check that the juices run clear. When the bird is cooked, allow to rest in the Lower Oven or next to the cooker for 15-30 minutes before carving.

SLOW ROASTING METHOD
(Main Oven, all models)
MAIN OVEN 180°C (350°F), GAS MARK 4

Season the bird and place into the Rayburn meat tin and prepare as for Fast Roasting. Hang the tin on the fourth set of runners in the Main Oven for the calculated time, basting occasionally. Turn the oven to a higher setting 30 minutes before the expected finishing time. The oven will then begin to rise in temperature ready for being quickly brought to a high setting to finish cooking roast vegetables and trimmings.

VERY SLOW ROASTING METHOD (CHICKEN ONLY)
(cast-iron Lower Ovens only)
MAIN OVEN 200°C (400°F), GAS MARK 6

It's also possible to finish cooking a chicken by slow roasting using a cast-iron Lower Oven. Season and prepare the bird as before and calculate the total cooking time for Fast Roasting. Hang the tin on the fourth set of runners in the Main Oven and allow 30 minutes for the bird to start to brown. Then transfer to continue to slow roast in the cast-iron Lower Oven for double the remaining cooking time. Return it to the Main Oven at the end of the cooking to crisp the skin if necessary before leaving it to rest.

POULTRY AND GAME ROASTING MATRIX
(For turkey and goose, see separate section)

	Main Oven 200°C (400°F), Gas Mark 6	FAST ROASTING TIMES
CHICKEN	900g (2 lb) 1.5kg (3 lb) 1.75kg (4 lb) 2.25kg (5 lb)	45-50 minutes 1-1$\frac{1}{4}$ hours 1$\frac{1}{2}$ hours 1$\frac{3}{4}$ hours
DUCK		1-1$\frac{1}{4}$ hours
GROUSE		30-35 minutes
PIGEON		20-35 minutes
PARTRIDGE		35-45 minutes
PHEASANT		45-60 minutes
QUAIL		12-15 minutes
SNIPE		12-15 minutes
WOODCOCK		12-15 minutes

Note: all cooking times are approximate

TURKEY ROASTING TIMES

If using a frozen bird, it is essential for safety reasons that you defrost it for the correct length of time. Leave in a cool room and allow a day for every 4.5kg (10 lb) of frozen bird.

Below are the suggested timings suitable for whole turkeys, turkey crowns (whole birds with legs removed) and special turkey roasts including; boned and rolled turkeys, saddles of turkey, butterflied turkey breasts, turkey ballontines and turkeys stuffed with ham or pheasant breasts. All cooking times are approximate.

FAST ROASTING METHOD
(Main Oven, all models)
MAIN OVEN 190°C (375°F), GAS MARK 5

Generously butter the breast with some soft butter and cover with some rashers of streaky bacon. Place in the meat tin, on a grill rack if liked, and roast un-trussed. Slide onto the lowest set of runners for an hour until nicely browned, then tent loosely with foil. Roast for 18 minutes per 450g (1 lb). When the turkey is nearly cooked, remove the foil to allow it to finish browning if necessary. As a guide, the total roasting times are listed below. 30 minutes before the finish time, turn the oven to a higher setting. This allows the oven to start to increase in temperature, ready for being quickly brought to a high setting to finish cooking vegetables and trimmings. This allows the bird time to rest and keep hot on or next to the cooker for up to an hour before carving, while you cook last minute green vegetables and finish making gravy.

TURKEY: FAST ROASTING TIMES

3.6-5.4 kg	8-12 lbs	$2^{1}/_2$-$3^{3}/_4$ hours
5.4-7.25 kg	12-16 lbs	$3^{3}/_4$-5 hours
7.25-9.0 kg	16-20 lbs	5-$6^{1}/_2$ hours
9.0-10.8 kg	20-24 lbs	$6^{1}/_2$-$7^{3}/_4$ hours
10.8-12.6 kg	24-28 lbs	$7^{3}/_4$-9 hours

Note: all cooking times are approximate

VERY SLOW ROASTING METHOD
(Main Oven, all models)
MAIN OVEN 150°C (300°F), GAS MARK 2

Prepare the bird as above, place in the meat tin, on a grill rack if liked, and roast un-trussed. Slide onto the lowest set of runners, tented loosely with foil. Roast according to the chart on the following page. Turn the oven to a higher setting 30 minutes before the expected finishing time. The oven will then begin to rise in temperature, ready for being quickly brought to a high setting to finish cooking roast vegetables and trimmings. Remove the foil from the turkey for the final 30 minutes to allow it to finish browning if necessary.

To check that the bird is thoroughly cooked, ideally use a meat thermometer in the thickest portion of the thigh – behind the knee joint next to the body. It should read 82-85°C (180-185°F). Alternatively, pierce with a skewer and check that the juices run clear. If any tinge of pink shows, return it to the oven and check again after 20 minutes. A further check is to shake hands with the legs – they should be easy to wiggle in their sockets and the thickest portion of the drumsticks should feel tender when pressed. Allow the bird to rest on the top plate or next to the cooker whilst making gravy using the cooking juices.

TURKEY: VERY SLOW ROASTING TIMES

3.6-5.4 kg	8-12 lbs	4-6 hours
5.4-7.25 kg	12-16 lbs	6-8$\frac{1}{2}$ hours
7.25-9.0 kg	16-20 lbs	8$\frac{1}{2}$-11 hours
9.0-10.8 kg	20-24 lbs	11-13$\frac{1}{2}$ hours
10.8-12.6 kg	24-28 lbs	13$\frac{1}{2}$-16 hours

Note: all cooking times are approximate

GOOSE ROASTING TIMES

Prepare the bird using the Fast Roasting Turkey Method (on the previous page) keeping it un-trussed. Do not prick the skin all over but do prick the heavy folds of fat just behind the wings by the back legs. Protect the legs and wings with fat bacon and foil to prevent burning. It is essential to roast a goose on a grill rack in a meat tin to allow the goose fat to drain away during cooking. Hang the tin on the fourth set of runners in the Main Oven. Roast for a total timing of 18 minutes per 450g (1 lb). A whole stuffed goose 4.5kg (10 lb) will therefore take approx. 3 hours total cooking time, a 5.4kg (12 lb) goose 3$\frac{1}{2}$ hours. After the first hour when it is nicely browned, remove the fat that has filled the tin, turn the bird upside down and tent the bird loosely with foil and roast for a further hour. Remove the fat again and turn back the right side up, covered, to finish cooking. Remove the foil for the last 20 minutes to brown the breast.

BONED AND ROLLED GOOSE ROASTS

For roasts such as 'goose banquet rolls', 'birds within a bird' (a pheasant in a chicken in a goose, etc.) and turkey or duck breasts rolled in a boned goose, fast roast using the turkey Fast Method timings as a guide. Since boned and rolled roasts are so dense it is essential to ensure that they are thoroughly cooked right to the centre. The use of a meat thermometer is strongly recommended. The slow method is not suitable for these roasts and should not be used.

BUTTERFLIED LEG OF LAMB BOULANGERE

SERVES 6-8
1.1-1.3kg (2^1/$_2$-3 lb) leg of lamb, butterfly cut
1.3kg (3 lbs) potatoes
1 large onion
15g (^{1}/$_2$ oz) butter
Salt and freshly ground black pepper
150ml (5 fl oz) vegetable or chicken stock

Ask your butcher for a butterfly cut of leg of lamb that has been trimmed of any surplus fat. Peel and thinly slice the potatoes and onion. Melt the butter in the meat tin and arrange a layer of potatoes over the base. Add some onion and seasoning. Continue layering the vegetables until all the potato and onion are used up and pour the stock over. Add the grill rack in the high position and place the lamb on top of this, fat side uppermost.

MAIN OVEN 180°C (350°F), GAS MARK 4
Slide the tin onto the fourth set of runners and roast for about an hour, depending on size, until the lamb is cooked to your liking. Transfer to rest in the warm and return the potatoes to the top of the oven to brown before serving.

AMERICAN POT ROAST

SERVES 6-8
1.82kg (4 lb) topside of beef, with a thin layer of fat
Salt and freshly ground black pepper
3 tbsp oil
1 medium onion, chopped
6 cloves of garlic, chopped
1 medium carrot, chopped
2 tbsp plain flour
450ml (15 fl oz) water
300ml (10 fl oz) red wine
1 bayleaf
450g (1 lb) pearl onions
6 large carrots, cut into small batons

Place the oil in a large casserole and heat on the boiling end of the hotplate. Season the meat and then brown it on all sides in the hot oil. Remove from the pan and set aside. Add the onion, garlic and the chopped carrot. Cook for a couple of minutes and then add the flour and cook for a further minute. Gradually add the liquids and once simmering, add the bayleaf. Return the meat to sit in the liquid.

MAIN OVEN 180°C (350°F), GAS MARK 4
Transfer, uncovered, to the middle of the oven and roast for 2 hours, turning the meat twice during this time. Blanch the pearl onions in boiling water for a minute, drain and plunge into cold water to release the skins. Peel the onions and prepare the carrots. After 2 hours, add the onions and carrot batons and stir into the sauce. Continue cooking until the vegetables are tender. Carve the meat into thick slices and arrange on a warmed platter. Taste and correct the seasoning of the sauce. Serve the vegetables and sauce around the meat and serve with plain boiled potatoes or simple mash.

BEEF AND CARROT CASSEROLE

SERVES 6
25g (1 oz) plain flour
Salt and freshly ground black pepper
675g (1^1/$_2$ lbs) braising steak
6 tbsp oil
1 large onion, chopped
1 clove of garlic, crushed
4 carrots, sliced
450ml (15 fl oz) beef stock

Mix the flour well with the salt and pepper and use to coat the meat (shaking in a polythene bag is the easiest way of doing this). Shake off the excess flour and discard. Heat the oil in a large cast-iron casserole on the boiling end of the hotplate and brown the meat in batches. Keep warm on a plate. Move the casserole to the cooler end of the hotplate, add the onion and cook until softening, turning from time to time. Return the meat to the pan and add the garlic and carrots with the stock. Bring to the boil and then simmer on the hotplate for 5 minutes.

MAIN OVEN 120°C (250°F), GAS MARK L-1
Ⓒ LOWER OVEN IN SLOW COOKING MODE
Transfer to the oven and cook for 3-4 hours until the meat is tender. Taste and adjust the seasoning.

KEN'S IRISH STEW

Ken makes the best Irish stew. Adding carrot is not strictly authentic, neither is adding a teaspoon of Marmite, but both add colour and flavour. The sliced potatoes are added early on so they cook and break down to thicken the stew naturally.

SERVES 4
8 to 12 middle neck lamb or mutton chops
1 tbsp vegetable oil
3 large onions, thinly sliced
900g (2 lb) old potatoes, half kept whole, half thickly
  sliced
450g (1 lb) carrot, cut into short batons (optional)
600ml (1 pint) lamb or vegetable stock
Salt and freshly ground black pepper
Chopped fresh parsley

Trim the meat of any excess fat. Heat the oil in a cast-iron casserole on the boiling end of the hotplate and fry the meat and onions in batches until nicely browned. Take the casserole off the heat and add the sliced potatoes and carrots, then add the stock to cover the meat and vegetables. Season, then cover with a tight fitting lid and bring to a gentle simmer.

MAIN OVEN 150°C (300°F), GAS MARK 2
Transfer to the middle of the oven and cook for 1$\frac{1}{2}$-2 hours. Add the whole potatoes so that they are mostly covered by the cooking liquid. Return to the oven and cook for a further 30-40 minutes. Taste, adjust the seasoning and add the parsley and serve.

VARIATION
LANCASHIRE HOTPOT

If you have the time, browning the chops in a little oil or dripping, before assembling, considerably improves the appearance of this comforting casserole.

SERVES 4
As for Ken's Irish stew (above) plus:
2 lambs' kidneys, skinned and sliced
250ml (9 fl oz) stock
25g (1 oz) butter

Follow the Irish stew recipe, omitting the carrots and slicing all of the potatoes thinly. It is not necessary to brown the meat and onions. Add the lambs' kidneys

and reduce the quantity of stock to 250ml (9 fl oz). Put a layer of potatoes, onions, kidney and chops into a casserole. Season lightly and then continue adding layers, finishing with a neat layer of potatoes. Pour over the stock. Melt the butter and brush it over the potatoes.

MAIN OVEN 160°C (325°F), GAS MARK 3
Cover and place in the middle of the oven for 2 hours. Remove the lid for the final 30 minutes to allow the potatoes to crisp and brown.

BEEF EN CROUTE

SERVES 6
900g (2 lb) beef fillet, cut from the centre of the fillet
Salt and freshly ground black pepper
55g (2 oz) butter
1 tbsp olive oil
2 large onions, finely sliced
85g (3 oz) mushrooms, sliced
A little freshly grated nutmeg
A pinch Marigold Swiss vegetable bouillon powder
175g (6 oz) smooth liver pâté
Salt and freshly ground black pepper
368g (13 oz) packet frozen puff pastry, thawed
Beaten egg, to glaze

Trim any fat from the fillet and tie it up at regular spaces along the joint using kitchen string to keep its shape. Season well with salt and pepper. Melt the butter and oil in a meat tin. Place the beef into the meat tin and roll it in the butter and oil.

MAIN OVEN 200°C (400°F), GAS MARK 6
Hang the tin on the top set of runners and cook for about 20 minutes turning the meat over once or twice until it has browned on all sides. Cook for 20 minutes for a rare to medium-rare finish (cook for 15-16 minutes if you prefer a rare result, or for 23-25 minutes if you like your meat well done). Do try it with the 20 minute timing given, as it really is best eaten this way.

Lift out onto a pre-chilled plate and place in a cool place to become completely cold. Add the sliced onions to the juices that have collected in the meat tin and return to the oven to cook for 8-10 minutes, stirring twice. When the onions are just turning a golden colour, add the mushrooms and cook for 3-4 further minutes. Remove from the oven, season with salt, pepper, nutmeg and Marigold powder. Leave to cool and then mix thoroughly with the liver pâté.

Roll out the pastry to a rectangle 35 x 40cm (14 x 16 inch) to fit the fillet. Place half the mushroom and liver duxelle mixture in the centre of the pastry. Remove the string and place the meat on top of the duxelle, flat side uppermost so that it will sit well when turned the right side up. Season well with salt and pepper. Cover the meat with the rest of the duxelle mixture. Brush the edges of the pastry with water. Fold the pastry around the meat and turn the ends in and tuck underneath so that all edges seal well and the join is on the underside. Turn upright and stand on a greased baking sheet or line with Bake-O-Glide.

Beat the egg with a pinch of salt and brush the pastry liberally with two coats. Cut strips and diamond shapes from the left-over pastry to make stalks and leaves. Mark with a knife and use to decorate the top of the pastry. Brush the decoration with egg wash. Chill in the refrigerator before baking. Remove and bring to room temperature 30 minutes before cooking. If preferred, the recipe can be prepared up to this stage a day ahead, in this case leave the brushing with egg wash until just before baking.

MAIN OVEN 200°C (400°F), GAS MARK 6
With the grid shelf on the fourth set of runners, cook for about 25 – 30 minutes until pale golden brown. Remove from the oven and allow to it to rest for 5-10 minutes on a warm platter before carving into slices. Serve with a good beef gravy and Béarnaise Sauce (*see* p94).

CASSOULET

SERVES 4-6
225g (8 oz) haricot beans
115g (4 oz) streaky bacon, chopped
450g (1 lb) belly pork, cut into chunks
225g (8 oz) garlic sausage
900ml (1¹/₂ pints) chicken stock
225g (8 oz) tomatoes, blanched, skinned and chopped
Bouquet garni or 1 bay leaf, parsley and thyme sprigs
Salt and freshly ground black pepper
115g (4 oz) fresh breadcrumbs

Wash the beans in cold running water, place in a pan, cover with cold water and leave to soak overnight. Rinse and cover with fresh water. Bring to the boil and

boil for 15 minutes. Place the bacon into a casserole with the belly pork and garlic sausage cut into 2.5cm (1 inch) cubes. Drain the beans and add to the casserole with the stock, tomatoes, bouquet garni and seasoning.

MAIN OVEN 160°C (325°F), GAS MARK 3
Mix well, cover and cook in the middle of the oven for 1¹/₂ hours. Remove the bouquet garni and add a little more stock if necessary. Sprinkle the breadcrumbs over the top and continue to bake uncovered for a further hour.

CROWN ROAST OF PORK

It's rather 70's but fun once in a while to have a crown roast. Ask your butcher to prepare a crown of pork from the loin cutlets. It is best to order in advance.

SERVES 8
1 crown of pork
Stuffing
1 onion, chopped
2 sticks of celery, chopped
55g (2 oz) bacon or pancetta, chopped
25g (1 oz) butter, melted
175g (6 oz) breadcrumbs
2-3 slices of pineapple fresh or tinned, chopped
2 tbsp fresh sage, chopped
85g (3 oz) chopped apricots
Salt and freshly ground black pepper
1 egg, beaten
Garnish
Watercress
Caramelised pineapple slices

Wrap foil around each cutlet bone – this will avoid the bones becoming charred during cooking. Place in the Rayburn meat tin with a ball of tin foil in the centre to keep the crown in shape.

MAIN OVEN 190°C (375°F), GAS MARK 5
Roast for 30 minutes per 450g (1 lb) plus 30 minutes.

Meanwhile make the stuffing. Fry the onion, celery and bacon in the melted butter until soft. Add to the breadcrumbs and mix in with the pineapple, sage and apricots. Season and bind together with the egg.

One hour before cooking is completed take out the ball of foil and replace with the stuffing. Return to the Main Oven and continue cooking.

Serve with the foil removed from the cutlet bones and garnished with watercress and pineapple slices. To caramelise the pineapple slices: melt some butter and sugar together and cook until just beginning to go golden, then add the pineapple and heat through until beginning to brown.

VARIATION
CROWN ROAST OF LAMB

Use 2 chined best-ends of neck of lamb.

MAIN OVEN 190°C (375°F), GAS MARK 5
Roast for 20 minutes per 450g (1 lb) plus 20 minutes.

FLEMISH BEEF CASSEROLE

SERVES 4
60g (2^1/$_4$ oz) butter
5 onions, sliced
800g (1^3/$_4$ lb) chuck/braising/stewing steak
115g (4 oz) kidney
115g (4 oz) liver
300ml (^{1}/$_2$ pint) dark beer
1 slice of bread spread with mustard
1 piece dark unsweetened chocolate

Melt the butter and fry the onions until lightly browned, remove from the pan and reserve. Cut the meats into 2^1/$_2$cm (1 inch) cubes and fry until brown. Place the onions and meats into a casserole, pour over the beer and add the slice of bread and the chocolate.

HOTPLATE
Bring to the boil then transfer to the Main Oven.

MAIN OVEN 140°C (275°F), GAS MARK 1
Place on the grid shelf on the fourth set of runners down and cook for about 3 hours.

Serve with any flavour of mash (*see* p74).

GLAZED PERRY HAM

This recipe was created after sampling award-winning Perry from Brook Farm, Wigmore, Herefordshire (01568 770562). For the best looking type of gammon joint, ask your butcher for a half-horseshoe cut.

SERVES 8
2kg (4^1/$_2$ lb) piece of gammon
750ml (1^1/$_2$ pints) dry perry (pear cider)
Water
1 onion, quartered
Handful of fresh parsley, stalks and heads
8 black peppercorns
Glaze
2 rounded tsp English mustard
2-3 tbsp Demerara sugar
Garnish
Maraschino cherries or cloves
Caramelised pear quarters

Place the gammon joint into a saucepan and cover with water, bring to the boil. Drain off all the water and rinse the meat. Replace the joint into the clean saucepan and pour over the perry, then top up with enough water to barely cover the meat. Add the onion, parsley and peppercorns. Cover with a lid and bring to the boil and simmer for 10 minutes.

HOTPLATE
Simmer on the hotplate for 20 minutes per 450g (1 lb) plus 20 minutes.

MAIN OVEN 140°C (275°F), GAS MARK 1
Alternatively use the oven. Bring to the boil.
Place on the lowest set of runners and simmer for about 3-3^1/$_2$ hours.

Remove the gammon from the liquid, cool a little and remove any string. Take a sharp knife and peel off the rind. Score the fat into a diamond pattern. Place the gammon onto a piece of Bake-O-Glide in the Rayburn meat tin then spread ready-made mustard thickly over the fat and press Demerara sugar all over the mustard.

MAIN OVEN 200°C (400°F), GAS MARK 6
Slide the tin into the centre of the oven and bake until the top is nicely browned, about 15-20 minutes.

Place on a serving dish and garnish the diamonds of fat with maraschino cherries (fixed with part of a cocktail stick) and/or cloves. Serve accompanied with caramelised pears, made by sautéing pear quarters in butter and sugar.

TIP! Serve with a parsley sauce made up from 55g (2 oz) each of butter and flour heated with 600ml (1 pint) of the strained cooking liquor, whisk continuously until thickened, and stir in 25g (1 oz) chopped fresh parsley.

HUNGARIAN BEEF GOULASH

The authentic way of cooking Goulash is by frying the meat in lard and this is an occasion where it's best to stick with the original recipe. Only use oil if you really need to.

SERVES 4
85g (3 oz) lard or sunflower oil
Salt and freshly ground black pepper
40g (1½ oz) plain flour
900g (2 lb) chuck steak or shin, cut into 55g (2 oz) pieces
400g (14 oz) onions, cut into rough chunks
2 cloves of garlic, crushed
2 tbsp paprika
1 x 400g can of chopped tomatoes
2 tbsp tomato purée
1 litre (1¾ pints) beef stock
150ml (¼ pint) sour cream
2 tbsp milk

Heat the lard or oil in a cast-iron casserole on the simmering end of the hotplate. Season the flour and use to coat the meat, (shaking in a polythene bag is the easiest way of doing this). Shake off the excess flour and move the casserole to the boiling end of the hotplate and fry the meat at a high temperature to brown. Avoid crowding the base to prevent the meat steaming rather than browning. Remove the meat and keep warm and add the onions, cooking until just starting to brown. Add a little more fat if necessary. As they start to brown, stir in the garlic and paprika, stirring for 1-2 minutes. Return the meat to sit on top of the onions and pour over the tomatoes, purée and stock.

MAIN OVEN 160°C (325°F), GAS MARK 3
Bring just to the boil then cover and transfer to the middle of the Main Oven and cook for about 1¼-1½ hours, until tender but not falling apart. Mix the sour cream with the milk and swirl into the goulash just

before serving. The remains of the dish can be extended to make a delicious soup with the addition of more tinned tomatoes and stock.

ONE PIECE GINGER BRAISED BEEF

SERVES 8
Take a piece of beef suitable for slow cooking – such as brisket or rolled rib, about 1.3kg (3 lb) in weight and fry off in a little oil, in a casserole. Add 6-8 shallots, fry to colour, then add 150ml (¼ pint) port or red wine, 2 or 3 pieces of root ginger about 1cm (½ inch) in length, 2 tbsp Worcestershire Sauce and black pepper. Heat the casserole on the hotplate for 5 minutes, and then transfer to the Main Oven at an idling temperature and leave to cook for 4-5 hours.

VARIATION
Replace the root ginger with 10 prunes.

SLOW-COOKED HARISSA LAMB

You will need to marinade the lamb the day before for this wonderful North African dish.

SERVES 6
2kg (4½ lb) leg of lamb
6 cloves of garlic, crushed
2 rounded tsp Harissa paste
2 tsp ground cumin
1 tsp paprika
1 tsp salt
Freshly ground black pepper

With a sharp knife cut the leg of lamb into diamonds, entering the meat to a depth of about 5 mm (¼ inch).

Make up a paste with the crushed garlic, Harissa, cumin, paprika, salt and black pepper. Smear this paste all over the leg of lamb and place in a large plastic bag and marinade in the refrigerator overnight.

Remove the leg of lamb from the plastic bag and place in a roasting tin, lined with Bake-O-Glide.

MAIN OVEN 220°C (425°F), GAS MARK 7
Place the tin just below the centre of the oven and

immediately turn the Main Oven to 120°C (250°F), Gas Mark L-1. Cook for 4-5 hours or even longer, the meat should come away from the bone easily.

Remove the meat from the oven, allow to rest for 10 minutes, and serve with couscous and a salad.

LAMB SHANKS

SERVES 4
2 tbsp olive oil
4 lamb shanks, approx. 225g (8 oz) each
16 small shallots, peeled
4 carrots, peeled and cut into chunks
1 stick of celery, chopped
2 cloves of garlic, crushed
1 x 400g can of chopped tomatoes
300ml ($^1/_2$ pint) red wine, such as Shiraz
1 tsp caster sugar
2 tbsp Worcestershire sauce
Salt and freshly ground black pepper
2 bay leaves
2 sprigs of fresh rosemary

Heat the oil in a large frying pan on the hotplate, and fry off the lamb shanks until they are browned on all sides. Remove with a slotted spoon and place in a cast-iron casserole. Gently fry the shallots, carrots, celery and garlic and place in the casserole over the lamb. Pour the tomatoes and wine into the frying pan, add the sugar, Worcestershire sauce, salt and pepper and bring to the boil, stirring to deglaze the pan. Pour over the lamb and vegetables. Tuck in the bay leaves and rosemary.

HOTPLATE
Bring the contents of the casserole to the boil.

MAIN OVEN 120°C (250°F), GAS MARK L-1 OR IDLING
ⓒ **LOWER OVEN IN SLOW COOKING MODE**
Transfer to the oven and cook for $2^1/_2$-3 hours or until the meat is falling from the bone.

When the lamb has cooked, remove it from the casserole along with the vegetables and keep warm in the Lower Oven. Turn up the cooker control and reduce the cooking liquid until it becomes a thick sauce, skim off any liquid fat. Return the lamb and vegetables to the sauce, heat through and serve with mashed potatoes or noodles.

SLOW-ROASTED BELLY PORK

SERVES 8-10
2kg ($4^1/_2$ lb) belly of pork, skin deeply scored
2 tsp Chinese five spice powder
Salt and freshly ground black pepper
50ml (2 fl oz) olive oil
2 large Bramley apples, peeled and chopped
Juice of $^1/_2$ a lemon
600ml (1 pint) light stock

Place the pork in the meat tin, fat side up. If the skin is at all wet, dry thoroughly using kitchen paper. Sprinkle the spice powder over the skin, and again generously with salt and pepper. Drizzle over the oil. Toss the apple in the lemon juice and arrange around the meat.

MAIN OVEN 160°C (325°F), GAS MARK 3
Hang the meat tin on the fourth set of runners and roast for 3-$3^1/_4$ hours. Remove to a warm platter to rest. Add the stock to the roasting tin and deglaze the cooking juices and cooked apple to make a rustic sauce. Slice the cooked pork; make sure everyone has a piece of crisp crackling. Serve with lots of creamed potatoes and a crisp green vegetable or stir-fry.

Right
Lamb Shanks

STEAK AND KIDNEY PUDDING

SERVES 6
350g (12 oz) ox kidney
900g (2 lb) stewing steak or shin
Salt and freshly ground black pepper
25g (1 oz) plain flour
1 large onion, finely chopped
A beef stock cube
A pinch Marigold Swiss vegetable bouillon powder
For the pastry
225g (8 oz) self raising flour
115g (4 oz) shredded beef suet
Cold water, to mix

Skin and clean the kidneys by cutting the rounded outsides in half and opening them inside out, pulling and cutting away the white cores. Cut each half into four pieces. Cut the beef into 2.5cm (1 inch) cubes. Mix the flour well with the salt and pepper and use to coat the meat, (shaking in a polythene bag is the easiest way of doing this). Shake off the excess flour and discard.

Sift the remainder of the flour into a bowl with a pinch of salt. Mix in the suet and add 6-8 tablespoons of water to make a soft dough. Roll into a circle and cut out a third to make a lid. Use the rest of the pastry to line a 1.4-1.7 litre (2½-3 pints) pudding basin. Fill with the beef and kidney, mixed with the onion. Crumble over the stock cube, add the Marigold powder and pour cold water to come within 2.5 cm (1 inch) of the top.

Roll out the remaining pastry into a circle and fix onto the edge of the pastry with a little water. Cover with a pleated disk of both baking parchment and foil and fix securely. Place on a trivet or small enamel plate in a saucepan and pour boiling water to come halfway up the side of the basin. Cover and bring to the boil. Adjust the position on the hotplate to maintain a medium boil for 30 minutes.

MAIN OVEN 120°C (250°F), GAS MARK L-1
Ⓒ LOWER OVEN IN SLOW COOKING MODE
Transfer to continue to steam for 3-4½ hours on the floor of the oven, no topping up will be necessary. Otherwise, continue steaming on the hotplate, topping up with boiling water periodically as needed.

VARIATION
STEAK AND KIDNEY PIE

SERVES 6
As for Steak and Kidney Pudding (above) plus
425ml (¾ pint) beef or vegetable stock
1 tbsp Worcestershire sauce
1 tbsp mushroom ketchup or soy sauce
2 tbsp chopped fresh parsley
Salt and freshly ground black pepper
For the pastry
280g (10 oz) packet frozen puff pastry, or 225g (8 oz)
  flour quantity of rough puff, flaky or shortcrust pastry
A beaten egg
A pinch of salt

Follow the Steak and Kidney Pudding filling recipe, but brown the floured meat in batches in 2-3 tbsp oil. Remove the meat and fry the onion until it just starts to brown. Stir in the remaining seasoned flour and gradually incorporate the stock, or use a proportion of stout. Finish by flavouring with the sauces, ketchup and parsley. Return the meat to the casserole, and season well. Simmer gently on the simmering end of the hotplate for 5 minutes.

MAIN OVEN 120°C (250°F), GAS MARK L-1
Ⓒ LOWER OVEN IN SLOW COOKING MODE
Transfer to cook in the oven for 2-3 hours until tender.

Taste and adjust the seasoning then turn the filling into a 1.2 litre (2 pint) pie dish and allow it to cool. Place a pie funnel in the centre. Roll out the pastry on a lightly floured surface to 3mm (⅛ inch) thick, in a shape a little larger than the pie dish. Cut 1cm (½ inch) strips of pastry (enough to cover the edge of your dish). Brush the strips with a little cold water and fix to the edge of the pie dish then brush over with water. Cover the pie with pastry and seal down, crimping the edge. Roll out any trimmings to make pastry leaves and use to decorate the top. Beat the egg in a cup with the salt and brush all over the pastry, giving two coats.

MAIN OVEN 200°C (400°F), GAS MARK 6
Bake on a grid shelf on the third set of runners for 20 minutes until the pastry is risen and golden. Then transfer to a grid shelf on the lowest set of runners and cook for a further 15-20 minutes, sliding in a cold plain shelf above to prevent over-browning.

VENISON CASSEROLE

500g (1lb 2oz) stewing venison, cubed
Marinade
140g (5oz) shallots, finely chopped
2 cloves of garlic, finely chopped
225g (8 oz) leek, sliced
125ml (4 fl oz) gin
500ml (18 fl oz) red wine
1 bay leaf
Salt and freshly ground black pepper
2 tbsp plain flour
Salt and black pepper
Olive oil

Place the venison into a glass bowl. Sprinkle over the shallots, garlic and leek. Pour over the gin and red wine, add the bay leaf and seasoning. Mix well and place in the refrigerator for 24 hours. During this time occasionally turn the meat in the marinade.

Remove the venison from the marinade, drain well. Place the flour in a large plastic bag with the salt and pepper. Shake the venison in the seasoned flour to coat each piece of meat.

Heat the olive oil in a frying pan, at the hot end of the hotplate, and fry the meat in batches until browned. Place into a casserole, add the marinade and bring the contents to the boil, stirring, cook until thickened.

MAIN OVEN 120°C (250°F), GAS MARK L-1
Ⓒ LOWER OVEN IN SLOW COOKING MODE
Then transfer to a slow oven for 3 hours until tender.

Serve with potato and celeriac mash, buttered sprouts and carrot batons.

WHOLE OVEN-BAKED GAMMON

Cooked slowly in the oven this is an ideal recipe to serve a crowd. For ease of cooking, get a cut to fit the meat tin – we've been known to take the meat tin to the butchers!

SERVES 25
1 whole gammon or ham, on the bone

Soak the gammon in cold water to remove excess salt, usually overnight. Remove from the water and rinse.

Line the Rayburn meat tin with two pieces of foil, set at right angles to each other. Place the meat on the foil. Gather the foil together but do not cover too tightly, make sure the edges are sealed well.

MAIN OVEN 160°C (325°F), GAS MARK 3
Bake the gammon for 20 minutes per 450g (1 lb). If you use a meat thermometer it should register 75°C when inserted in the thickest part, avoiding contact with the bone.

GLAZING
The gammon can be glazed with any one of the following suggestions:
• Honey and chopped almonds.
• Mustard and Demerara sugar.
• Marmalade.

If glazing the gammon: half an hour before the finish of the calculated cooking time turn the Rayburn up to 220°C (425°F), Gas Mark 7. Then remove the meat from the oven, carefully open the foil and remove the meat and place it on a board – (save any juices which can be used as flavouring, or the fat for making savoury pastry or frying). Strip the rind away from the fat and use a sharp knife to score the fat into diamond shapes. Smother with the desired glaze and put back into the meat tin.

Return to the hot oven and cook for the remaining time, until the glaze has nicely browned. Allow the meat to rest before carving for about 30 minutes. Serve with a Cumberland or plum sauce.

PLUM SAUCE

1kg (2 lb 4 oz) plums
225g (8 oz) Demerara sugar
300ml (¹/₂ pint) clear vinegar
¹/₂ tsp salt
8 cloves
Pinch of cayenne pepper
Pinch of ground ginger

Roughly chop the plums and place in a large pan (no need to remove the stones). Add the sugar, vinegar, salt, cloves and spices. Place on the hotplate, heat to dissolve the sugar then bring to the boil and simmer for 30 minutes.

Strain through a sieve and rub through as much plum pulp as possible. Reheat and simmer until the sauce thickens to the consistency of double cream, serve hot or cold.

DUCK BREASTS WITH DAMSON SAUCE

SERVES 4
4 duck breasts
4 tsp balsamic vinegar
Sauce
450g (1 lb) damsons
55g (2 oz) sugar
4 tbsp malt vinegar
300ml (1/2 pint) red wine or port
Salt and freshly ground black pepper
Garnish
Watercress

To make the sauce: in a saucepan on the hotplate, cook the damsons with the sugar, vinegar and red wine until the damsons are soft. Strain through a sieve and rub through as much damson pulp as possible. Reheat and simmer until the sauce is the consistency of double cream. Keep warm in the Lower Oven.

Wipe the duck breasts. Then place them, skin side up, on the grill rack in the Rayburn meat tin (place a piece of Bake-O-Glide in the base of the meat tin to make washing-up easier). Slash the skin of each duck breast three times, without cutting into the flesh. Brush with the balsamic vinegar.

MAIN OVEN 220°C (425°F), GAS MARK 7
Slide the meat tin onto the second set of runners down and grill for about 20-25 minutes, basting twice with the balsamic vinegar.

Remove the cooked duck breasts from the oven and allow them to rest for 5 minutes. Cut each duck breast into slices and serve drizzled with some of the sauce and garnished with watercress. Serve the remaining sauce separately.

CHICKEN BREASTS IN PANCETTA WITH GARLIC CREAM

SERVES 6
Another excellent recipe for entertaining as it can be prepared up to a day ahead. The pancetta helps to keep the breast meat moist and succulent.

6 boned free-range chicken breasts
140g (5 oz) garlic cream cheese, e.g. Boursin
Salt and white pepper
12 slices pancetta
A little soft butter
300ml (10 fl oz) dry white wine
1 tsp cornflour
200ml (7 fl oz) full-fat crème fraîche
1 tbsp chopped fresh parsley or coriander

Remove the skin from each of the chicken breasts. Using a sharp knife, cut a pocket lengthways across each breast and spread half the garlic cream cheese in the centre of each. Season very lightly with salt and more generously with white pepper. Wrap each breast neatly in two slices of pancetta. Lightly butter the base of a baking dish and arrange the assembled chicken breasts inside.

MAIN OVEN 200°C (400°F), GAS MARK 6
Slide the baking dish on a grid shelf on the second set of runners at the top of the Main Oven. Bake for 12-15 minutes, depending on size, until starting to colour (if browning too quickly, transfer to the floor of the oven towards the end of this period).
Once browned and cooked through, transfer to a warmed serving dish and keep hot in the Lower Oven.

To make the sauce: add the wine to the baking dish and return to the oven for five minutes to dissolve the cooking juices. Pour into a small saucepan and add the rest of the cheese. Mix the cornflour in a cup with a little cold water and whisk into the sauce, heat gently on the simmering end of the hotplate. Stir in the crème fraîche and taste and adjust the seasoning. Just before serving stir in the chopped fresh herbs. Serve each portion with a little of the sauce to coat. Serve the rest to hand.

Right
Chicken Breasts in Pancetta with Garlic Cream

MRS TWEEDY'S CHICKEN AND LEEK PIE

SERVES 4
900g (2 lb) cold cooked chicken
425ml (15 fl oz) milk
15 threads of saffron
55g (2 oz) butter
450g (1 lb) leeks, fresh or frozen
25g (1 oz) butter
1 clove of garlic, crushed
55g (2 oz) flour
A little chicken stock or jelly
1 x 295g can of Campbell's Chicken and White Wine Condensed Soup
Salt and white pepper
150ml (5 fl oz) double cream
3 tbsp chopped fresh tarragon or parsley
450g (1 lb) puff pastry
1 egg
A pinch of salt

Place the milk in a pan or Pyrex jug with the saffron and place in the Lower Oven to warm. If using fresh leeks, wash well and chop thinly. Melt half the butter and add the leeks and cook on the simmering end of the hotplate for 7-10 minutes, stirring until softened. Remove using a slotted spoon and keep hot in the Lower Oven. Add the remaining butter to the pan and stir in the garlic for a minute. Add the flour and cook for 3-5 minutes, stirring all the time. Gradually add the warmed milk, whisking after each addition. Now add the turkey stock or jelly and soup. Taste and adjust the seasoning. Finally, add the cream and herbs and a little more milk, if necessary, to achieve a medium-thick coating sauce.

Cut the chicken into bite-size chunks and stir into the sauce with the softened leeks. Turn into a large pie dish. Roll out the pastry and cut enough strips to attach to the edge of the dish with water. Place a pie funnel in the centre, and brush the strips with water. Cover with the remaining pastry and crimp the edges. Whisk the egg in a cup with a good pinch of salt and brush the pastry. Roll and cut decorative shapes from the trimmings and give a second coating of egg wash.

MAIN OVEN 200°C (400°F), GAS MARK 6
Bake on the grid shelf on the fourth set of runners for 25-40 minutes until golden.

GINGER AND APRICOT THAI TURKEY

SERVES 6
900g (2 lb) cold cooked turkey
450g (1 lb) left-over ham, diced or 225g (8 oz) lightly smoked bacon bits
115-175g (4-6 oz) block of creamed coconut
300ml (1/2 pint) chicken stock
1/2 tsp curry powder
1 x 295g can of Campbell's Condensed Mushroom Soup
200g (7 oz) plain yoghurt
Juice of 1 lemon
175g (6 oz) ready-to-eat dried apricots
140g (5 oz) stem ginger, chopped
2 bananas (not-too-ripe), to accompany

In a pan on the simmering end of the hotplate, soften the coconut with the chicken stock and curry powder. Keep hot. If using bacon, place it in a dry pan on the simmering end of the hotplate to allow the fat to run, then move it to the boiling end or the floor of a hot oven. Leave to cook, stirring a couple of times. Once cooked, remove with a slotted spoon to a baking dish and leave to cool. Cut the apricots and add them to the pan, along with the stem ginger cut into small pieces. Then add the condensed soup, yoghurt, half the lemon juice, and a little of the ginger syrup. Mix all together and add the cut up turkey and ham or bacon pieces. Turn into a baking dish.

MAIN OVEN 200°C (400°F), GAS MARK 6
Cook on a grid shelf on the lowest set of runners for about 50-60 minutes, until completely heated through and bubbling. If it starts to brown too quickly, slide a cold plain shelf above. Serve with rice and salad. Cut up the banana and sprinkle with the remaining lemon juice, serve as an accompaniment.

FISH AND SEAFOOD

Any method of cooking fish can be achieved successfully with the Rayburn. However, one particular advantage of using the Main Oven is that cooking smells are directed, to the outside, so fishy odours are kept to an absolute minimum in the kitchen.

Below is a guide to cooking methods and timings. Timings will vary depending on the size and thickness of the fish. Fish should not be over-cooked, so test for 'doneness' sooner rather than later! A fine skewer inserted into the thickest part of the fish should penetrate easily and the flesh should flake. A general 'rule of thumb' is to allow 10 minutes per 2.5cm (1 inch) of thickness. (*See the 'General guide to cooking times for fish' chart, opposite.*)

As with cooking in general, a certain amount of personal taste and choice can, and should, be exercised!

GRILLING
Fish can be grilled in either of two ways; either by using a ridged grill pan on the hotplate or on the grill rack in the meat tin at the top of a hot Main Oven.

USING A GRILL PAN Heat the grill pan and lightly oil the fish before placing it into the hot grill pan. Press the fish down onto the ridges and cook until it changes colour and has the characteristic brown stripes, then turn over and cook the other side. This method is most suitable for the more 'robust' fish such as salmon steaks or fillets, mackerel, halibut, herring, tuna, swordfish, trout.

TO OVEN GRILL Set the Main Oven to 230-240°C (450-475°F) Gas Mark 8-9, lightly oil the fish or dot with butter and place on the grill rack in the Rayburn meat tin. Slide the tin onto the top or second set of runners. Although this method is suitable for almost all types of fish it lends itself to the more delicate fillets of fish, such as plaice, sole, kippers, smoked haddock, sardines or for whole flat fish. A sprinkle of paprika on white fish will add colour.

FRYING

SHALLOW-FRYING This takes place in a frying pan with a small amount of oil, or a mixture of oil and butter. This can be undertaken on the hotplate or, if the Main Oven is hot, it can be started on the hotplate and then transferred to the floor of the Main Oven to finish. An ideal frying pan to use is a completely cast-iron one or one that has a removable handle. It can then be used both on the hotplate and in the oven. The oil should be hot before the fish goes into the pan, so that cooking starts immediately. This quick method is suitable for almost all types of fish, especially fillets. Shallow frying will take about 4-10 minutes, depending on the thickness of the fish.

DRY-FRYING Oily fish can be cooked this way in a non-stick frying pan.

DEEP-FRYING This is done in a heavy-based pan on a high temperature hotplate. Take care – do not leave the pan unattended or indeed do not fill the pan more than a third full of oil. Deep-frying should always be undertaken on the hotplate, the pan can be moved to a higher or lower temperature, as required. A thermometer is recommended to ensure the oil is at the correct temperature for the food; too cool and the fish will absorb oil, too hot and the fish will be cooked on the outside but not in the centre. For this method the fish should always have a coating such as crumbs or batter. The oil should be at a temperature of 190°C (375°F), fry until golden brown and drain on kitchen paper.

STIR-FRYING This is a fast way of cooking fish and is best carried out in a flat-based wok, or a broad-based heavy sauté pan. Place the pan on a hot hotplate and turn up the Rayburn control knob to high. As with any stir-frying, the fish should be cut into strips. This method is most suitable for the more robust firm-fleshed fish, such as monkfish.

POACHING
This is a method of cooking fish by immersing in simmering, seasoned liquid. It can be done in a shallow pan or fish kettle on the hotplate. Stock (court-bouillon) or milk make the best poaching liquids. If you are going to make a sauce use a mixture of wine and stock for the poaching liquid.

For larger fish or a number of fillets, poach in the Rayburn meat tin in the Main Oven. The oven temperature should be moderate to high, dependent upon what else is cooking. If necessary, cook for slightly longer times at a lower temperature.

GENERAL GUIDE TO POACHING
Fillets are poached for 5-10 minutes.
$1^1/_2$-$1^3/_4$kg whole salmon about 18-20 minutes.

Fish can also be poached in oil. This method is suitable for firm-fleshed fish, such as halibut or salmon. Cover the fish fillets in oil and place the pan on the hotplate on a low heat, slowly bring up to a temperature of 60°C (140°F), test with a thermometer. Poach for about 15 minutes; – the fish will be firm when cooked. Remove the pan from the heat and drain well.

POACHING A LARGE SALMON Wrap the salmon in buttered foil and place in the Rayburn meat tin. Pour boiling water around the foil-covered fish so that it comes half way up the fish. Carefully slide onto the centre set of runners. Cook – according to the weight guidelines in the 'Poaching a large salmon' chart, *below* – at 220°C (425°F) Gas Mark 7:

General guide to cooking times for fish	
Fillets – thin	5-8 minutes
Fillets – thick	9-12 minutes
Whole small fish – round	8-12 minutes
Whole fish – flat	8-10 minutes

Poaching a large salmon		
1kg	(2 lb 4 oz)	about 10 minutes
1.5kg	(3 lb 5 oz)	about 18 minutes
2kg	(4 lb 8 oz)	about 23 minutes
2.5kg	(5 lb 8 oz)	about 28 minutes
3kg	(6 lb 8 oz)	about 30 minutes
4.5kg	(10 lb)	about 35 minutes

ROASTING

Roasting or baking fish uncovered in the oven is a simple and effective way of cooking fish and it leaves the skin easy to strip away from the succulent flesh. Oily fish does not need any extra oil or butter.

Open-roasting fish takes place in the Main Oven at a high heat – 200°C (400°F) Gas Mark 6 to 240°C (475°F) Gas Mark 9.

WHOLE FISH The fish should be cut diagonally through the skin to help even cooking. Whole fish can be roasted, either stuffed with herbs or, on a bed of tomatoes, peppers and spring onions, mixed with a little olive oil placed underneath the fish. (Start the vegetables roasting for 10 minutes before adding the fish.) Cook for 15-30 minutes, depending on the size and thickness of the fish – a thicker fish will take longer to cook than a thinner one, four fish will take a few more minutes than one.

FILLETS Thick fillets, such as salmon, trout, cod and haddock will take about 8-10 minutes to cook. White fish should be lightly oiled or dotted with a little butter.

BAKING

Fish can be baked in the same way as open-roasting, but at a lower temperature, 180°C (350°F) and therefore for a longer time. For example, fish steaks take about 25 minutes. This method of cooking at a moderate heat very often fits in with cooking a meal. For example, Mediterranean vegetables can be roasting at the top of a hot Main Oven at the same time as fish baking on the centre set of runners below.

Fish can be baked wrapped in foil, or parchment, to form a parcel, (*en papillote*). Thinly sliced vegetables can be added for flavour. This method is particularly found in Chinese and Far East cookery. Fish can also be baked in coarse salt or pastry, (*en croute*).

STEAMING

Steaming cooks fish by hot moisture, rather than liquid. It can take place either on the hotplate or in the oven.

The hotplate method requires either a steamer, (use a flavoured stock), or the fish can be steamed between two greased heatproof plates. Fillets will need 15-20 minutes according to thickness, for thick cuts of fish such as steaks allow up to 30-35 minutes.

Oven-steaming either takes place within a 'parcel', (*see* Baking above), or the fish can be placed in a greased dish and covered in foil to steam in the oven. Again the oven temperature can be variable, as long as it is 180°C (350°F) Gas Mark 4 or above.

BOUILLABAISE

This is a wonderful Mediterranean fish soup. It's a delightful dish to share with friends.

SERVES 4-6
For the base
1 tbsp olive oil
1 onion, finely chopped
$^1/_2$ bulb of fennel, sliced
3 cloves of garlic, crushed
300ml ($^1/_2$ pint) white wine
450g (1 lb) fish bones, from white fish and shellfish
1 bay leaf
6 peppercorns, crushed
water
For the soup
2 shallots, very finely chopped
A pinch of saffron threads
$^1/_2$ bulb of fennel, sliced
4 sweet tomatoes, deseeded and chopped
1 tbsp Pernod
450g (1 lb) mixed white fish, such as halibut, sea bass, monkfish, John Dory, gurnard, whiting
350g ($^3/_4$ lb) shellfish, mussels, clams, prawns
Salt and freshly ground black pepper
2 tbsp chopped parsley
Juice of 1 lemon
To serve
Fresh bread or toasted
Rouille

Heat the oil in a large saucepan and gently fry the onion, fennel and garlic for about 3-4 minutes. Add the wine and bring to the boil and boil rapidly to reduce the wine by half. Add the fish bones, bayleaf and peppercorns and enough water to cover. Return to the boil and then slide the saucepan to the simmering side of the hotplate and simmer for 30 minutes – or place in a moderate Main Oven to simmer.

Strain the base stock, return it to a clean saucepan and add the shallots. Reheat to simmering point and add the saffron, fennel, tomato and Pernod, bring up to the boil. Add the fish and shellfish with those pieces that need cooking the longest going into the pan first. (Discard any mussels that refuse to open). Simmer until all the fish is cooked – about 15 minutes in all, season and add the parsley and lemon juice. Serve the soup in bowls with bread, and rouille, (a red, piquant mayonnaise) in a separate dish.

For a simple rouille: place 4 cloves of garlic, 3 egg yolks, 175g (6 oz) roasted red peppers, 1 red chilli and salt into a food processor. Whiz together and slowly drizzle in 225ml (8 fl oz) of olive oil.

MONKFISH AND BACON BROCHETTES

SERVES 4
6 rashers thinly cut smoked streaky bacon
450g (1 lb) monkfish, cut into 16 cubes
1 large red pepper, cut into 12
12 fresh bay leaves
For the glaze
2 tbsp soy sauce
3 tbsp Chilli Jam (see p93)

Stretch the bacon with the back of a knife and cut the rashers in half. Thread chunks of monkfish onto skewers alternating with bacon rolls, red pepper and fresh bay leaves.

MAIN OVEN 220°C (425°F), GAS MARK 7
Place on the grill rack in the Rayburn meat tin and brush with a mixture of soy sauce and Chilli Jam. Grill at the top of the oven for 10 minutes, then turn the skewers over, brush with more soy and Chilli Jam and return to the oven to complete cooking.

MOREISH KEDGEREE

SERVES 4
450g (1 lb) undyed thick smoked haddock fillets
225g (8 oz) long grain or basmati rice
1 tsp Marigold Swiss vegetable bouillon powder
4 free-range eggs
115g (4 oz) butter
A small onion, finely chopped
1 tbsp Madras curry paste
4 tbsp mango chutney
Juice of $^1/_2$ a lemon
1 tsp cayenne pepper
Sea salt and freshly ground black pepper
Plenty of chopped fresh parsley, to taste

Right
Bouillabaise

Place the fish in a baking dish with a few tablespoons of water, cover with foil and bake in a hot Main Oven for 8-12 minutes, until just cooked. Allow to cool and then remove the skin and break into flakes.

Cover the rice with 2.5cm (1 inch) water and add the bouillon powder. Bring to the boil and then transfer to the simmering end of the hotplate and cook until just tender. Drain through a sieve and run cold water over the rice for about a minute, to rinse away any excess starch.

Place the eggs in a pan of cold water and bring to the boil, simmer for 10 minutes. Run them under cold water until completely cold, and then shell and cut into eighths.

Melt the butter in a large pan and add the onion. Cook on the simmering end of the hotplate until softened. Stir in the curry paste and cook for a minute. Stir in the rice, mango chutney, lemon juice and cayenne. Taste and adjust the seasoning, and then carefully fold in the flaked fish and eggs. Serve piping hot with the parsley sprinkled over.

TIP! If preferred, allow all the ingredients to become cold before mixing, and then reheat in a hot Main Oven when wanted, adding the parsley at the last minute.

VARIATIONS
- Use fresh salmon to make a delicious salmon kedgeree.
- As a store cupboard standby: substitute canned salmon for fresh using most of a 418g can of pink salmon. Pour the juices from the tin into the sauce, before removing the skin and bones.
- With all versions, if a more risotto-like consistency is preferred, 150ml (1/4 pint) of single cream can be stirred into the mixture before adding the parsley to make a creamier sauce.

PEPPERED TUNA STEAK

SERVES 4
2-4 tbsp cracked black peppercorns
4 x 175g (6 oz) yellowfin tuna steaks
A little sea salt
425ml (15 fl oz) dry white wine
2 cloves of garlic, crushed
2 tbsp butter

With the hotplate at a high setting, pre-heat a cast-iron grill pan on the simmering side and, once hot, transfer to the boiling end to absorb the full amount of heat. Remove the fish from the refrigerator 30 minutes before cooking. Press the cracked pepper into both sides of the tuna and season with a very little salt. Set a plate to warm in the Lower Oven. Place the steaks onto the ridges of the grill pan and cook for 1½-2 minutes on each side, until rare in the centre, or opaque throughout, if you prefer. Transfer to the warm plate and leave to rest on the top plate.

Off the heat, add the wine, garlic and butter to the grill pan. Return to the hotplate and boil for 2-3 minutes, until reduced to 150ml (5 fl oz). Spoon over the steaks and serve immediately.

PRAWNS PIRI-PIRI

SERVES 4
2 mild red chillies, or more to taste
4 cloves of garlic
350g (12 oz) softened butter
1 tbsp Tabasco sauce
900g (2 lbs) king prawns (with shells and heads on)
Juice of 1 lime
4 tbsp chopped fresh coriander
To serve
lime wedges

Pound the chillies and garlic together. Add to the butter with the Tabasco sauce and mix well. This is more easily made in a food processor.

With a sharp, serrated knife split the prawns down the back to reveal the black vein and carefully remove it with the knife tip. Rinse them in a bowl of cold salted water and then dry with kitchen paper. Generously spread the garlic butter down the back. If you prefer serving them without their shells, peel the body carapace away, leaving the head and tail attached, and smear the butter here. Any surplus butter can be frozen for up to a month.

Two hours before cooking, place in a bowl and add the lime juice. Stir until they are all coated with the juice, cover and refrigerate. Bring to room temperature 30 minutes before cooking and place the prawns in overlapping rows in the meat tin or a baking tray.

MAIN OVEN 200°C (400°F), GAS MARK 6
Grill at the top of the oven for 3-5 minutes or so until just cooked, use a spoon to baste the prawns with the butter and juices. For smaller quantities; heat a cast-iron frying or grill pan on the hotplate until hot, then add the prawns and cook on a grid shelf at the top of the oven. Scatter with the chopped coriander and serve immediately with the lime wedges and plenty of crusty bread to mop up all the chilli and garlic butter.

SEAFOOD PAELLA

SERVES 6
2 tbsp olive oil
1 large onion, finely chopped
1 clove of garlic, crushed
450g (1 lb) paella rice such as Calaspara
A good pinch of saffron
1 large glass of dry white wine
900ml (1^1/$_2$ pints) chicken or vegetable stock
4 large tomatoes, skinned, quartered and de-seeded
2 red peppers, de-seeded and diced
225g (8 oz) mussels, scrubbed and de-bearded
225g (8 oz) clams
225g (8 oz) cooked shell-on prawns
A few small squid, cleaned and sliced
6 scallops
6 cooked King prawns
Juice of ^{1}/$_2$ a lemon
Chopped fresh parsley
Salt and freshly ground black pepper
Lemon wedges to garnish

Heat the oil in a large shallow pan and gently fry the onion for 2-3 minutes to soften. Next, add the garlic and rice, turn the rice in the pan until all the grains have been coated in oil and have started to become translucent.

Place the saffron in a cup with a little of the warmed stock to infuse. Add the wine to the pan and almost all of the stock. Add the tomatoes and peppers. Cover with a lid and cook partially offset on the simmering end of the hotplate for 8 minutes. Stir and add the mussels, clams and the saffron liquid. Replace the lid and cook fully on the simmering end of the hotplate for 4 minutes. Next add the prawns, squid and scallops. Stir to gently cook the squid and scallops and to heat through the prawns. Add the lemon juice and parsley, taste and adjust the seasoning, adding the remainder of the stock if necessary. Garnish and serve.

SALMON EN CROUTE WITH A WHITE WINE AND MUSHROOM SAUCE

SERVES 8
1.5kg (3 lb) salmon in two fillets, skinned
Juice of ^{1}/$_2$ a lemon
Salt and freshly ground pepper
1 packet frozen ready-rolled puff pastry sheets, thawed
1 egg, beaten
Sauce
115g (4 oz) mushrooms, sliced
150ml (^{1}/$_4$ pint) white wine
Salt and freshly ground black pepper
425ml (^{3}/$_4$ pint) double cream
Garnish
Lemon wedges
Watercress

Firstly make the sauce; place the mushrooms in a pan with the wine and seasonings and simmer on the hotplate for 5 minutes. Remove the mushrooms and reduce the wine to about 3 tbsp by boiling rapidly. Add the cream and simmer until thickened, return the mushrooms to the cream sauce. Cool.

Remove any bones from the salmon and sprinkle over the lemon juice. Season. Put one sheet of pastry onto the plain shelf, lined with Bake-O-Glide. Place one salmon fillet on the sheet of pastry, cover with 3 tbsp of the sauce then place the other salmon fillet on top. Brush the pastry with beaten egg, to make a seal, place the other sheet of pastry on top. Pinch the pastry together and brush with the egg glaze all over. Mark 'scales' on the pastry using the tip of a spoon.

MAIN OVEN 190°C (375°F), GAS MARK 5
Slide the shelf onto the centre set of runners and cook for about 30 minutes, until the pastry is golden brown. Transfer the plain shelf to the floor of the Main Oven for 4-5 minutes to brown the base well.

Meanwhile, heat the sauce and place it in the Lower Oven to keep warm. Serve the salmon cut into slices with the sauce as an accompaniment. Garnish with lemon and watercress.

SALMON FILLETS WITH RASPBERRY SAUCE

A main course with the all the great tastes of summer, and with no extra fat added – it's healthy too!

SERVES 4
4 salmon fillets
Sprigs of fresh dill
Sauce
140g (5 oz) fresh raspberries
2 tbsp raspberry vinegar, made up to 150ml ($^1/_4$ pint)
  with water
2 tsp redcurrant jelly
Salt
Garnish
Whole raspberries
4 lemon wedges

First make the sauce. Place the raspberries, raspberry vinegar and water into a saucepan. Cover and bring to the boil on the hotplate, then simmer for 10 minutes.

Pass the raspberry sauce through a sieve, return it to the pan and boil rapidly to reduce, until only 150ml ($^1/_4$ pint) remains, this takes about 3 minutes. Then add the redcurrant jelly, dissolve and season. Keep warm in the Lower Oven.

MAIN OVEN 220°C (425°F), GAS MARK 7
To cook the salmon: place the fillets onto a piece of Bake-O-Glide, placed on a baking tray. Scatter with the sprigs of dill. Cook for about 8-10 minutes on the second or third set of runners until the salmon is just cooked in the centre.

Remove the dill sprigs. Arrange the salmon on four plates. Drizzle sauce over the salmon and serve any remainder separately. Garnish with a few whole raspberries and a wedge of lemon. Serve hot with new potatoes and mange-tout peas.

TROUT IN PERNOD

SERVES 2
2 tbsp flour
Salt and freshly ground black pepper
2 trout, cleaned and prepared
85g (3 oz) butter
175g (6 oz) mushrooms, sliced

1 clove of garlic, crushed
2 tbsp Pernod
2 tbsp Dijon mustard
Garnish
Watercress

Place the flour in a large plastic bag and add the seasonings, put the prepared trout into the flour and shake well to coat. Melt the butter in an ovenproof frying pan, heat and add the trout.

HOTPLATE
Cook the fish over a high heat for 4-5 minutes, then carefully turn over and cook the other side.
ALTERNATIVELY
MAIN OVEN 220°C (425°F), GAS MARK 7
Transfer the trout to the floor of the oven to cook, turn over after 5 minutes and cook the other side.

Transfer the trout to a serving dish and place in the Lower Oven to keep warm. Place the frying pan back on the hotplate and fry the mushrooms and garlic in the trout juices for 3-5 minutes. Stir in the Pernod and mustard, add a little water if the sauce is too thick. Pour the sauce over the trout and serve garnished with watercress.

ROASTED SEA BASS

When open-roasting fish the skin goes hard, meaning it can be easily removed, revealing the moist flesh below. Whole trout or salmon can also be cooked this way.

SERVES 4
4 sea bass
Fresh herbs such as parsley, dill
2 lemons
Sea salt

Prepare the whole fish and slash the flesh three times on each side. Place the fish on a piece of Bake-O-Glide in the Rayburn meat tin. Fill the cavities of the fish with a selection of fresh herbs and 2 lemons, cut into halves.

MAIN OVEN 220°C (425°F), GAS MARK 7
Slide the tin onto the second set of runners and open roast for about 20-25 minutes, check for doneness – if the flesh flakes, it is cooked.

Serve garnished with lemon and fresh herbs.

Right
Roasted Sea Bass

THAI CRAB CAKES

SERVES 4
40g (1^1/$_2$ oz) cream crackers
450g (1 lb) fresh white crabmeat
2 tbsp chopped parsley
1 egg, beaten
2 tbsp mayonnaise
1 tbsp English mustard powder
1 tbsp lemon juice
1 tsp Worcestershire sauce
4 tbsp butter
1 tbsp sunflower oil
Salt and freshly ground white pepper

Crush the crackers to fine crumbs by placing in a plastic bag and bashing with a rolling pin. Put the crab meat into a bowl with the parsley and add just enough of the cracker crumbs to absorb any moisture from the crab. Break the egg into a small bowl and whisk in the mayonnaise, mustard, lemon juice, Worcestershire sauce and some generous seasoning. Stir this into the crab meat but avoid breaking up any lumps of crab. Shape the mixture into 16 x 4cm (1^1/$_2$ inch) patties and place on a plate, cover and chill for an hour.

Heat the butter and oil in a large frying pan on the simmering end of the hotplate. Adjust the pan on the hotplate to give a medium heat and cook the cakes in batches for 2-3 minutes on each side, until crisp and richly golden. Keep warm until they are all cooked then serve immediately.

MAIN OVEN 200°C (400°F), GAS MARK 6
Alternatively, heat the fat in a shallow baking tray and bake near the top of the oven, turn after 4 minutes. Cook for a further 4 minutes until just cooked.

Serve the crab cakes immediately, with a dipping sauce.

DIPPING SAUCE
150ml (5 fl oz) rice vinegar
150g (5 oz) caster sugar
3 red chillies, finely sliced

To make the sauce: heat the vinegar and sugar in a small pan and simmer for 3 minutes, until reduced slightly and syrupy. Stir in the chillies and refrigerate.

TWEED KETTLE FISH PIE

SERVES 6
450g (1 lb) white fish fillet
450g (1 lb) undyed smoked fish fillet
1 medium onion, finely chopped
4 black peppercorns
1 bay leaf
700ml (1^1/$_4$ pint) milk
85g (3 oz) butter
85g (3 oz) plain flour
Salt and freshly ground black pepper
Juice of ^{1}/$_2$ a lemon
150ml (5 fl oz) single cream
225g (8 oz) cooked prawns, peeled
4 tbsp chopped fresh parsley
For the mash
1.5kg (3 lb) floury potatoes
85g (3 oz) butter
30ml (1 fl oz) milk

Place the fish, skin side down, in a baking dish. Add the onion, peppercorns and bay leaf and pour over the milk. Place in a hot Main Oven and cook for 15-20 minutes, until just cooked. Remove from the poaching liquid and leave to cool on a plate.

Melt the butter in a saucepan and add the flour. Stir on the simmering side of the hotplate for 1-2 minutes, and then gradually add the hot strained milk to make a smooth sauce. Season with a little salt and plenty of pepper and add the lemon juice, cream and parsley.

Skin and flake the fish and turn into a baking dish, scatter over the prawns. Pour the sauce over the fish and chill in the refrigerator. Boil the potatoes until just tender and then allow to drain thoroughly. Mash with the butter and milk and pipe or pile onto the fish mixture.

MAIN OVEN 180°C (350°F), GAS MARK 4
Bake in the centre of the oven for 30-40 minutes, until piping hot and the top is crisp and golden.

MAINLY VEGETABLES

Vegetables can be cooked in many different ways on and in the Rayburn. Place in a covered saucepan of water only just deep enough to cover the vegetables. Water boils quicker on a rising heat, so turn the cooker control up to the high position to get heat into the hotplate quickly. Once boiling, turn to the setting required for the oven temperature. The Rayburn's heat-graduated hotplate allows you to easily slide the saucepan or cooking vessel to the heat required. Generally, green vegetables are best cooked quickly on the hotplate to retain their colour.

Stir-frying is also easy on the hotplate; use a flat-based hard anodised wok or a large sauté pan. This is an ideal way for cooking green vegetables, such as pak choi.

The ovens can be used to steam, roast, braise and casserole root and Mediterranean vegetables. Aubergine slices can be brushed with oil and grilled at the top of a hot Main Oven, ideal for Moussaka because it helps make the dish less oily.

BEETROOT

BOILED

(Using the hotplate.) Cut off the leaves to within an inch of the top, wash and simmer for about 1 hour until tender. Remove from the water and cool a little, then peel off the skin.

FOR AN ACCOMPANIMENT TO COLD MEAT

Simply slice and cover with vinegar.

OVEN BAKED

Prepare the beetroot as for boiling, then wrap each beet in foil and place in a moderate oven to cook for about an hour or until tender.

ROASTED

Peel young raw beetroot and toss in olive oil and roast in a hot Main Oven.

BEETROOT IN A BALSAMIC CREAM SAUCE Ⓥ

Beetroot is delicious served as a hot vegetable.

SERVES 4-6
450g (1 lb) medium-sized beetroot, cooked
25g (1 oz) butter, melted
3 tbsp balsamic vinegar
3 tbsp crème fraîche
Salt and freshly ground black pepper
Garnish
Chopped fresh parsley

Cut the beetroot into quarters and place into a pan with the melted butter. Heat through and add the Balsamic vinegar and crème fraîche. Stir, and reheat until the sauce thickens slightly. Serve sprinkled with the chopped fresh parsley. Good with grilled pork chops.

BROCCOLI WITH ALMONDS Ⓥ

SERVES 4
450g (1 lb) broccoli
Salt and freshly ground black pepper
Juice of $\frac{1}{2}$ a lemon
40g ($1\frac{1}{2}$ oz) butter
40g ($1\frac{1}{2}$ oz) flaked almonds
1 clove of garlic, crushed

Cut the broccoli into even-sized florets and boil or steam until tender. Drain and place on a warm plate, season and squeeze over the lemon juice.

Meanwhile, melt the butter and sauté the almonds until just browning, add the garlic and cook for a further 2 minutes. Pour the sauce over the broccoli and serve.

VARIATION

• Substitute cauliflower florets for the broccoli.

FLAGEOLET BEANS Ⓥ

Delicious served with roast lamb.

SERVES 6
450g (1 lb) dried flageolet beans, soaked overnight
Honey mustard vinaigrette
3 tbsp cider vinegar
4 cloves garlic, creamed
Salt and freshly ground black pepper
1 tbsp wholegrain mustard
2-3 tsp clear honey
2-3 tsp fresh tarragon, chopped
6 tbsp hazelnut oil
6 tbsp olive oil

Cook the beans until tender, (according to packet instructions), usually about $1\frac{1}{4}$ hours. Bring to the boil and either continue to cook on the hotplate or transfer to the Main Oven at a moderate heat.

Whisk the vinaigrette ingredients together and pour some over the warm beans. (Keep any remaining dressing in a screw-top jar in the refrigerator.) Serve warm, or cover and leave to marinade for several hours and serve at room temperature.

GLAZED ONIONS ⓥ

SERVES 4

450g (1 lb) button onions, peeled
55g (2 oz) butter
3 tbsp caster sugar

Parboil the onions and drain. Melt the butter in a pan and add the sugar, then add the onions. Cook gently on the hotplate turning the onions over regularly in the glaze until they are golden and tender.

STIR-FRY GREEN BEANS WITH TOASTED SESAME SEEDS ⓥ

SERVES 4

450g (1 lb) French beans
1 tbsp sesame seeds
3 tbsp oil
1 clove of garlic, finely chopped
1 tbsp lemon juice
Salt and freshly ground black pepper

Top and tail the beans and boil for five minutes. If using frozen, boil for two minutes. Drain the beans and pat dry.

Toast the sesame seeds in a dry pan for a few moments until they begin to colour and pop. Add the oil and heat for one minute. Add the beans, garlic, lemon juice and seasoning. Serve.

JANSSON'S TEMPTATION

SERVES 4-6

2 onions, thinly sliced
25g (1 oz) butter
1kg (2 lb 4 oz) potatoes, cut into julienne strips
1 x 100g tin of anchovies
Freshly ground black pepper
300ml ($1/2$ pint) cream
2 tbsp breadcrumbs
2 tbsp grated cheese

In a frying pan, add half the butter and soften the onions. Butter an ovenproof dish and put in half of the potatoes. Cover with the onions and anchovies, season with the pepper. Put the remainder of the potatoes over the top.

Pour over any oil left from the anchovies, then the cream. Season again and sprinkle with the breadcrumbs and cheese.

MAIN OVEN 190°C (375°F), GAS MARK 5
Place the dish on the grid shelf in the centre of the oven and cook for about 45-55 minutes, or until the potatoes are tender and the surface is nicely browned.

LEEK, GINGER AND RED PEPPER STUFFED FLATTIES ⓥ

These can be prepared in advance, then chilled and cooked when required.

SERVES 6

6 flat mushrooms
25g (1 oz) butter
1 tbsp olive oil
Topping
25g (1 oz) butter
140g (5 oz) prepared leeks, sliced
55g (2 oz) white breadcrumbs
2 roasted red peppers (from a jar), chopped
1 cm ($1/2$ inch) fresh root ginger, grated
Salt and freshly ground black pepper
Garnish
Roasted cherry vine tomatoes

Wipe the mushrooms and trim the stalks. Melt the butter and oil in a frying pan on the boiling side of the hotplate and fry the base of the mushrooms, until just browned, (about 2 minutes). Place on a shallow baking tray, lined with Bake-O-Glide.

For the topping: melt the butter in the frying pan and sauté the leeks until soft but still retaining their colour. Place in a basin. Add the breadcrumbs, red pepper, ginger and season. Mix well together and divide the mixture between the mushrooms. Place the cherry tomatoes, brushed with a little oil, onto the baking tray.

MAIN OVEN 220°C (425°F), GAS MARK 7
Bake for about 15 minutes until golden brown.

LEEK AND GRUYERE TART ⓥ

SERVES 6
175g (6 oz) shortcrust pastry or use a ready-rolled
frozen shortcrust pastry circle (thawed)
25g (1 oz) butter
450g (1 lb) leeks, thinly sliced and washed
Salt and freshly ground black pepper
1 clove of garlic, crushed
300ml ($^1/_2$ pint) single cream
3 eggs
$^1/_2$ tsp nutmeg
115g (4 oz) Gruyère cheese, grated

Line a 20cm (8 inch) flan dish with the pastry. Melt the butter in a saucepan; add the leeks, salt, pepper and garlic. Cook until soft, about 15 minutes. Cool.

Beat the cream with the eggs, nutmeg and 85g (3oz) of the cheese. Place the leeks in the flan case and pour over the cheese mixture. Sprinkle the remaining cheese over the top.

MAIN OVEN 200°C (400°F), GAS MARK 6
Place the quiche on the floor of the oven and cook for about 30-35 minutes.

Serve warm or cold.

STEAMED CARROTS ⓥ

Carrots can be cooked on the hotplate as normal. However, the oven-steaming method below leaves you more room on the top of the Rayburn and produces a perfect result, without constant attention. This method of cast-iron Lower Oven cooking is great for when the Main Oven is in use.

SERVES 4
450g (1lb) carrots cut into batons or sticks
Salt
Garnish
Chopped fresh parsley

Place the carrots in a saucepan and barely cover with water, add salt to taste. Bring the carrots to the boil and simmer for 3-5 minutes on the hotplate, then drain off all the water.

Ⓖ **LOWER OVEN IN SLOW COOKING MODE**
Place the covered saucepan into the cast-iron Lower Oven to steam, about 20-25 minutes. Serve garnished with the chopped fresh parsley.

ORANGE STEAMED CARROTS ⓥ

SERVES 4
450g (1lb) carrots cut into batons or sticks
Juice and rind of 1 orange
15g ($^1/_2$ oz) butter
Garnish
Chopped fresh parsley

Method as above, but after draining the water add the orange juice and rind. Transfer to the floor of the Lower Oven for 20-25 minutes. Add the butter to the pan, shake and serve at once garnished with the chopped fresh parsley.

VARIATIONS

CARAWAY SEED CARROTS ⓥ

Cook 450g (1 lb) carrots using the Lower Oven method as above. After draining off the water, add a knob of butter and a sprinkling of caraway seeds before transferring to the Lower Oven to cook – about 20-25 minutes.

TARRAGON STEAMED CARROTS ⓥ

Cook 450g (1 lb) carrots using the Lower Oven method as above. When cooked, add 1 tbsp of crème fraîche and 1 tsp chopped tarragon to the pan, swirl around and serve.

Right
Leek and Gruyère Tart

MASH FACTORY Ⓥ

SERVES 4
675g (1¹/₂ lbs) floury potatoes, peeled
25g (1 oz) butter
125ml (5 fl oz) milk
A little cream (optional)
Salt and freshly ground black pepper

Cut the potatoes into even-sized pieces. Bring the potatoes to the boil in cold, salted water on the boiling side of the hotplate and then adjust the pan on the hotplate so that they continue to slow boil for 20-30 minutes, until tender.

Ⓒ LOWER OVEN IN SLOW COOKING MODE
Alternatively, after five minutes simmering, drain, cover and transfer to the oven for 20-30 minutes.

Drain and return the pan to the simmering side to dry off any excess moisture.

Pass the potatoes through a potato ricer or use a masher until completely smooth. Move the potato to one side of the pan and to this exposed side, add the butter and milk. Add the cream, if using, and season well. A little freshly grated nutmeg used sparingly is a good addition with some of the variations below. Place the edge of the pan on the hotplate, so that the liquids only, are heated on the hotplate. Once hot, beat or whisk into the potato until it is all light and fluffy. Taste and re-adjust seasoning if necessary.

VARIATIONS Ⓥ

CELERIAC MASH
Cook 50:50 with celeriac for 45-60 minutes and then add butter and chives.
COLCANNON
Butter, milk and add finely chopped cooked cabbage or young nettles.
CHAMP
Butter, milk or cream and add finely chopped spring onions.
CLAPSHOT
Cook 50:50 with swede for 45-60 minutes and add butter and chives.
MUSTARD MASH
Add butter and wholegrain mustard.
PARSLEY MASH
Add butter and plenty of freshly chopped parsley.
PUNCHNEP
Cook 50:50 with turnip for 45-60 minutes and add butter and chives.

ROAST POTATOES

SERVES 6
900g (2 lb) large, floury potatoes such as Desirée, King Edward or Maris Piper, peeled
Lard, dripping or fat from the roast or vegetable shortening and oil

Bring the potatoes to the boil in cold, salted water and gently parboil for 5-10 minutes, until they are just becoming soft around the outside, but not falling apart. Drain in a colander and wait for the steam to subside. Roast in a mixture of two fats, one from the meat being roasted, (this will give the potatoes an excellent flavour to compliment the meat). Otherwise, use half vegetable shortening and half oil.

MAIN OVEN 220°C (425°F), GAS MARK 7
Heat your chosen fat or oil in a baking tray or tin on the floor of the Main Oven until good and hot. Add the par-boiled potatoes and turn them in the hot fat so that they are well basted. Roast potatoes should be cooked on the floor of the Main Oven and can be finished off near the top of the oven to complete their browning. If cooking several trays, rotate them so they all enjoy a spell on the floor and at the top of the oven.

BAKED POTATOES Ⓥ

1 baking potato per person

Wash or wipe the potatoes and prick with a fork or skewer. Rubbing a little oil on the skin slightly shortens the cooking time.

MAIN OVEN 200°C (400°F), GAS MARK 6
Place on a tray or directly on a grid shelf in the top half of the oven and bake for 1-1¹/₄ hours. If baking more than one tray, swap the trays and allow a longer cooking time. If in a hurry, cut large potatoes in half, lengthways, to speed their cooking.

GRATIN DAUPHINOISE Ⓥ

Most authorities on food insist that a genuine Quiche Lorraine shouldn't include cheese, and there are many who insist the same for Gratin Dauphinoise. However, by all means add some, grated, if you would like to ring the changes, either between some of the layers or sprinkled on top or both.

SERVES 4
Soft butter
2 cloves of garlic, crushed
675g (1$^1/_2$ lb) potatoes, sliced thinly
Salt and freshly ground black pepper
Nutmeg, freshly ground
Milk
Double cream
Cheese, optional

Butter a large gratin dish liberally and then wipe with the garlic. Slice the potatoes, using, in order of preference, a mandoline, sharp knife or food processor. Reserve enough of the neatest slices for the top layer and then pack in the potatoes. Season each layer, lightly, with the nutmeg and salt and pepper. Pour over enough milk to almost cover the potatoes, then spread a thin layer of cream over the surface.

MAIN OVEN 190°C (375°F), GAS MARK 5
Bake for about an hour until the potatoes are tender, the liquid has been absorbed and there is a rich golden skin. This is an extremely forgiving dish, and can be cooked for varying times at other oven temperatures. Once cooked it can be kept hot in the Lower Oven for a long time, tightly covered with foil, until wanted.

VARIATIONS
POMMES BOULANGERE

Follow the Dauphinoise method, but start by softening 225g (8 oz) thinly sliced onions in a little butter and oil. Layer the potatoes with the onions and season generously. Pour over enough stock to just cover and bake in the same way.

POMMES LYONNAISE Ⓥ

Slice equal quantities of potatoes and onions thinly, then cook in a little butter and oil, stirring until the onions have softened and the potatoes have cooked and have turned golden. This dish can be baked in a baking dish in a hot Main Oven whilst cooking another dish. By doing this, you can avoid having to keep turning the mixture.

POMMES SAVOYARDE

Follow the Boulangère method, but also include diced pieces of bacon or ham in the layers, top with grated cheese.

SWISS ROSTI POTATOES Ⓥ

SERVES 4
675g (1$^1/_2$ lbs) potatoes
175g (6 oz) butter
1 medium onion, peeled and grated
Salt and freshly ground pepper

Scrub the potatoes and place in a pan, pour over enough boiling water to just cover. Add a teaspoon of salt and boil slowly for about 7 minutes. Drain well and allow to cool for 10 minutes. Melt 55g (2 oz) of the butter in a small pan, add the onion and soften for 5 minutes, stirring from time to time. Grate the potatoes by hand into a bowl, add the onions and season well.

Melt the remaining butter in a frying pan, preferably cast iron, on the simmering end of the hotplate. Using half the mixture and a 7.5cm (3 inch) biscuit cutter as a mould, pat down four piles to make cakes in the pan. Adjust the pan on the hotplate to give a moderate temperature and fry for 6-8 minutes until golden brown. Turn with a palette knife and fry the other side. Keep hot in the Lower Oven while you make a second batch. Alternatively, you can make a large Rösti in a pan and then cut this into wedges to serve.

HASSLEBACK POTATOES Ⓥ

Hasselbacken is the name of a famous Swedish restaurant in Stockholm where this delicious twist on roast potatoes was created.

SERVES 4
8 potatoes, each approx. 85g (3 oz)
55g (2 oz) melted butter
Salt and freshly ground black pepper

Peel the potatoes; place on a cutting board and cut a narrow slice from the bottom of each potato and discard, this will prevent the potato from rolling. Place on a chopping board with two wooden spoon handles on each side of the potato, lengthwise. Use a sharp knife and slice across, every 5mm ($^1/_4$ inch). The wooden spoon handles will prevent the knife from cutting entirely through the potato to produce a fanned potato effect. After you have cut the potatoes, drop them into the cold water until ready to cook them. Drain the potatoes and pat dry. Place in a lightly buttered baking dish and brush the melted butter liberally over the potatoes making sure it runs down the fanned slices.

MAIN OVEN 220°C (425°F), GAS MARK 7
Roast, uncovered, near the top of the oven for 40-50 minutes, brushing again with more melted butter halfway through cooking. These can also be cooked at a lower temperature for a longer time if necessary, move to the top of the oven to finish browning.

PARMESAN PARSNIPS Ⓥ

SERVES 6
675g (1$^1/_2$ lbs) medium-sized parsnips
Beef dripping or olive oil
55g (2 oz) Parmesan, grated

Bring the parsnips to the boil in cold salted water and gently parboil for 10-12 minutes, until they are just tender. Drain well in a colander.

MAIN OVEN 220°C (425°F), GAS MARK 7
Heat the fat or oil in a tin in the oven until hot, and then add the parsnips, turning to evenly coat in the fat.

Roast anywhere in the oven, moving them to a higher position towards the end of their cooking to allow them to brown. Five minutes before they are ready, carefully drain away the cooking fat and discard. Dredge with the Parmesan and toss them so that they are evenly covered. Return to the oven to crisp for a few minutes.

ROASTED MEDITERRANEAN VEGETABLES Ⓥ

SERVES 4
2 courgettes, sliced
1 aubergine, diced
1 red onion, cut into chunks
5 cloves of garlic, peeled
2 red peppers, cut into squares
Fresh thyme
Freshly ground black pepper
Olive oil
Sea salt, optional

Place all the vegetables into a bowl and mix together with the sprigs of thyme, seasoning and enough olive oil to coat them. Transfer to the Rayburn meat tin, lined with Bake-O-Glide.

MAIN OVEN 220ºC (425°F), GAS MARK 7
Slide the tin onto the top set of runners.
Turn the vegetables occasionally and cook for about 30 minutes, or until the vegetables are tender and just beginning to brown around the edges.

Serve piping hot, sprinkled with sea salt, if liked.

TIP! Any left over vegetables can be used as a filling for a quiche or an omelette.

ROASTED WINTER ROOT VEGETABLES Ⓥ

SERVES 4
2 potatoes, peeled
2 parsnips, peeled
2 carrots, peeled
Half a celeriac, peeled
6 shallots, peeled
Fresh thyme or rosemary
Freshly ground black pepper
Olive oil
Sea salt, optional

Cut the potatoes, parsnips, carrots and celeriac into 2cm ($^3/_4$ inch) cubes. Halve the shallots.

Place all the vegetables into a bowl and mix well together with the sprigs of thyme or rosemary, seasoning and enough olive oil to coat them. Transfer to the Rayburn meat tin, lined with Bake-O-Glide.

MAIN OVEN 220ºC (425°F), GAS MARK 7
Slide the tin onto the top set of runners and cook for about 30 minutes or until the vegetables are cooked and just beginning to brown around the edges. Turn the vegetables occasionally during cooking.

Serve piping hot, sprinkled with sea salt crystals, if liked.

ROAST SWEETCORN Ⓥ

Roast corn on the cob (complete with their silky outer covering) for 15 minutes in a hot oven. Remove from the oven and strip away the covering, serve with melted butter.

TOMATO AND COURGETTE TART Ⓥ

SERVES 6
Pastry
115g (4 oz) plain flour
115g (4 oz) wholemeal flour
115g (4 oz) butter
Water to mix, approx. 4 tbsp
Filling
4 tomatoes, sliced
4 courgettes, sliced

3 eggs
200ml (7 fl oz) single cream
2 tbsp parsley, chopped
Salt and freshly ground black pepper
55g (2 oz) cheese, grated

Place the flours and butter into a bowl and rub in the butter until the mixture resembles breadcrumbs, or use a food processor. Add enough water to form firm dough. Roll out and line a ceramic 23cm (9 inch) flan dish.

Arrange the tomatoes and courgettes in the flan case. Beat together the eggs, cream, parsley and seasoning and pour over the vegetables. Sprinkle with the cheese.

MAIN OVEN 200°C (400°F), GAS MARK 6
Place the tart on the floor of the oven and cook for about 30-35 minutes. Serve cold with salad.

WATERCRESS SOUFFLE Ⓥ

SERVES 4
40g (1$^1/_2$ oz) butter
40g (1$^1/_2$ oz) plain flour
300ml ($^1/_2$ pint) milk
1 tsp English mustard
Salt and freshly ground black pepper
4 eggs, separated
125g (4$^1/_2$ oz) Cheshire cheese, grated
1 bunch of watercress or 1 packet

Take 15g ($^1/_2$ oz) of butter and grease a 1.7 litre (3 pint) soufflé dish.

Place the remaining butter, flour and milk into a saucepan. Bring to the boil, continuously whisking, and simmer until thickened. Add the mustard and seasonings.

Remove from the heat and beat in the egg yolks. Then stir in the cheese. Chop the watercress and add to the mixture. Whisk the egg whites until stiff and fold in. Place the mixture into the soufflé dish.

MAIN OVEN 180°C (350°F), GAS MARK 4
Cook in the centre of the oven for about 40-45 minutes, until well risen and golden. Serve immediately.

TIP! This soufflé could also be cooked in individual in ramekin dishes (allow a shorter cooking time).

LUNCHES AND SUPPERS

This section consists of an invaluable collection of dishes suitable as a single course.

CHICKEN AND CASHEW STIR-FRY

SERVES 3-4
2-3 chicken fillets, sliced into pencil thin strips
2 cloves of garlic, sliced
1 piece fresh ginger, sliced
1 tbsp soy sauce
3 tbsp sesame oil
1 red pepper, sliced
1 green pepper, sliced
1 bunch spring onions, sliced diagonally
115g (4 oz) mushrooms, sliced
225g (8 oz) beansprouts or noodles
75g (3 oz) cashew nuts
Salt and freshly ground black pepper

Place the chicken into a basin, add the garlic and ginger. Stir in the soy sauce and leave to marinate in the refrigerator.

HOTPLATE

Heat the sesame oil in a Rayburn wok. Once hot, add the chicken and stir-fry for a minute.

Then add the peppers and onions, stir-fry for two minutes. Add the mushrooms, bean sprouts and cashew nuts and stir-fry for a further minute. Season and serve at once.

FAST CHICKEN CAESAR SALAD

You'll need a cast-iron grill pan to cook the chicken with perfect grill stripes.

SERVES 4
4 free-range chicken fillets, approx. 140g (5 oz) each
2 tbsp olive oil
2 cloves of garlic, crushed
Croûtons
3 slices white bread, cubed
1 tbsp olive oil
25g (1 oz) butter
1 clove of garlic, crushed
Salad and garnish
1 cos lettuce, washed
*4-6 tbsp of a good Caesar salad dressing, such as
   Mary Berry's*
Shavings of Parmesan cheese

Trim the chicken of any fat and place in a glass bowl with the olive oil and crushed garlic to marinate for up to 1-2 hours.

HOTPLATE

Heat the cast-iron grill pan on the simmering side, then slide over to the hottest side and heat for a further 2-3 minutes. Remove the chicken fillets from the marinade and place them in the grill pan. Cook for about 4-6 minutes until the chicken has been 'branded'. Turn the chicken over and continue to cook for a further 8-10 minutes or, if the Main Oven is hot, transfer to the floor of the oven to complete the cooking.

Whilst the chicken is cooking, make the garlic croûtons; melt the olive oil with the butter and garlic, add the cubes of bread and shake to coat with the garlicky mixture. Gently fry until golden.

Break the lettuce leaves into bite-size pieces and toss with the Caesar salad dressing. Place in the salad bowl and serve topped with the warm, sliced chicken fillets. Garnish with the croûtons and shavings of Parmesan.

EASTERN LAMB CASSEROLE

SERVES 4
450g (1 lb) lean lamb, cubed
1 tsp ground cinnamon
1 tsp ground coriander
1 tsp cumin seeds
2 tsp olive oil
1 onion, finely chopped
1 garlic clove, crushed
1 x 400g (14 oz) can of chopped tomatoes
2 tsp tomato purée
125g (5 oz) dried apricots
250ml ($^1/_2$ pint) stock
Salt and freshly ground black pepper
Garnish
Fresh coriander

Right
Fast Chicken Caesar Salad

Place the lamb into a basin and add the spices and oil and mix well. Heat a non-stick cast aluminium casserole on the hotplate and add the spiced lamb. Cook for 4-5 minutes on the hottest side, until browned. Remove the lamb, using a slotted spoon and place to one side.

Then cook the onion, garlic, tomatoes and tomato purée for about 4 minutes, season to taste. Return the meat to the casserole and add the apricots and stock. Bring to the boil and simmer for 5 minutes.

MAIN OVEN 120-140°C (250-275°F), GAS MARK 1
Ⓒ LOWER OVEN IN SLOW COOKING MODE
Transfer to the oven for 1¹⁄₂-2 hours, until the meat is tender.

Serve garnished with roughly chopped fresh coriander.

FRANKFURTER SLICE

A Rayburn 'hot dog', supplied by Trisha Dunbar, is a rich scone base, topped with frankfurters and a piquant sauce. Made in the meat tin it serves a crowd of youngsters. This recipe is quite tolerant and can be moved around in the hot oven according to what else may be cooking.

SERVES 16
400g (14 oz) self raising flour
Salt to taste
175g (6 oz) butter
200g (7 oz) strong Cheddar cheese, grated
Approx. 150ml (¹⁄₄ pint) milk
1 large onion, or 2 medium onions, peeled and sliced
1 large pack of 20 frankfurters
2 tbsp English ready-made mustard
4 tbsp tomato ketchup
1 tbsp piquant brown sauce

Line the Rayburn meat tin with Bake-O-Glide.

Sieve the flour and salt into a bowl and rub in the butter, or use a food processor. Add two-thirds of the cheese and mix to a soft dough with the milk. Press the mixture evenly into the tin.

Cover the onion with water and boil for a minute or two, then drain off the liquid.

Arrange the frankfurters in lines over the scone dough.

Stir the mustard, ketchup and brown sauce together and spread over the frankfurters. Sprinkle over the blanched onion and then the remaining cheese.

MAIN OVEN 200-220°C (400-425°F) GAS MARK 6-7
Slide the tin onto the runners towards the top of the oven and bake for about 40 minutes until nicely browned, turning the tin half way through cooking.

Serve hot cut into slices with salad.

TIP! Use a mixture of cheeses, such as Windsor Red and white cheese for more effect.

GOATS' CHEESE, TOMATO AND BASIL TARTLETS ⓥ

SERVES 4
1 sheet ready-rolled puff pastry
115g (4 oz) goats' cheese
Fresh basil leaves
6-8 cherry tomatoes, sliced
Salt and freshly ground black pepper

Cut the puff pastry into squares. On each square place some goats' cheese and top with a basil leaf and slices of tomato.

MAIN OVEN 220°C (425°F), GAS MARK 7
Cook for about 15 minutes, towards the top of the oven until risen and browned.

Serve warm with a dressed bistro salad.

VARIATIONS
• Spread some pesto over the pastry before adding the cheese.
• Omit the goats' cheese and use extra tomatoes.
• Place roasted vegetables on the puff pastry squares and lay slices of Mozzarella cheese over.

GRILLED BURGERS WITH ROASTED RED PEPPER AND AVOCADO SALSA

SERVES 4
3 red peppers
Burgers
450g (1 lb) best quality minced beef
1 onion, finely chopped
1 clove of garlic, crushed
1 small chilli, finely chopped
2 tbsp fresh coriander, chopped
1 egg, beaten
Salt and freshly ground black pepper
Salsa
2 ripe avocados
Juice of 2 limes or 1 lemon
1 red onion, finely chopped
3 tbsp coriander, chopped
3 tomatoes, chopped finely
Salt and freshly ground black pepper
To serve
Pitta bread

Firstly, prepare the peppers for roasting; wash and cut in half, remove the core and seeds.

MAIN OVEN 220°C (425°F), GAS MARK 7
Place the peppers, skin side up, on the grill rack in the Rayburn meat tin, line the tin with Bake-O-Glide, (making washing up easier!). Grill at the top of the hot oven for about 10-15 minutes by which time the skins should have blistered, begun to turn brown and loosened from their flesh. Leave to cool.

Next make the burgers; place the beef into a bowl and add the onion, garlic, chilli, coriander and egg, mix well. Season. Form the mixture into 8 burgers and place on the grill rack in the meat tin. Slide the tin onto the top set of runners in the hot oven and grill for 10-15 minutes, turning over once.

Put the pitta bread into the oven on the lowest set of runners for about 5 minutes to heat through.

Make the salsa. Skin and chop the cooled peppers. Cube the avocado and cover with the lime juice, add the peppers, onion, coriander and tomatoes, season to taste. Split the pitta breads down the side and tuck in a burger. Serve accompanied by the salsa.

LANCASHIRE AND ROCKET QUICHE Ⓥ

SERVES 6
1 x 20cm (8 inch) flan dish
1 x frozen ready-rolled shortcrust pastry circle, thawed
1 x 50g packet rocket
225g (8 oz) Lancashire cheese, cubed
3 eggs
300ml ($\frac{1}{2}$ pint) single cream
3 tbsp chopped, fresh parsley
Salt and freshly ground black pepper

Line a 20cm (8 inch) flan dish with the pastry. Place the rocket and cubed cheese onto the base.

Beat the eggs with the cream, add the parsley and seasoning. Pour this over the rocket and cheese.

MAIN OVEN 200°C (400°F), GAS MARK 6
Place on the floor of the oven to cook for about 25-30 minutes, until golden brown and set. If necessary, move the quiche up to the oven grid shelf, set on the third set of runners, to brown the top of the quiche.

Serve warm or cold.

LINGUINE WITH CRAB

SERVES 4
350g (12 oz) linguine
3 tbsp olive oil
2 cloves of garlic, finely chopped
1 red chilli, deseeded and finely chopped
Grated zest of 1 lemon
280g (10 oz) crabmeat
4 spring onions, sliced
200ml carton of single cream or crème fraîche
Juice of $\frac{1}{2}$ a lemon
Salt and freshly ground black pepper
Garnish
Chopped fresh parsley

Cook the linguine according to packet instructions.

Meanwhile, heat the oil in a large diameter frying pan and gently fry the garlic, chilli and lemon zest until soft but not brown. Add the crabmeat, spring onions, cream and lemon juice. Simmer until heated through.

Drain the linguine and place in pasta bowls, spoon the crab mixture over the top and garnish with the parsley. Serve at once.

MACARONI WITH TWO CHEESES Ⓥ

SERVES 4
Cheese sauce
425ml (15 fl oz) milk
1 bay leaf
4 black peppercorns
25g (1 oz) butter
25g (1 oz) plain flour
1 tbsp English mustard powder
Salt and freshly ground white pepper
A little freshly grated nutmeg
115g (4 oz) grated Gruyère, Mature Cheddar or
  Lancashire cheese
55g (2 oz) grated Parmesan
150ml (5 fl oz) double cream
Pasta
350g (12 oz) macaroni
Salt
1 large onion, finely chopped
Butter for greasing

Place the milk, bay leaf and peppercorns in a small pan or Pyrex jug in the Lower Oven to warm 30 minutes before making the sauce. Strain.

Melt the butter in a pan on the simmering end of the hotplate and stir in the flour and mustard powder. Gradually incorporate the strained milk to make a smooth sauce. Season. Add nutmeg and half of the two cheeses. Take off the heat and stir in the cream.

Drop the macaroni into a large pan of salted water and add the onion. Cook the pasta for 8 minutes or according to the packet. Drain the pasta and onion through a colander. Add to the sauce, stir well and then place in a buttered baking dish. Scatter over the remaining cheese.

MAIN OVEN 200°C (400°F), GAS MARK 6
Bake in the middle of the oven for 20-30 minutes, until piping hot and with a golden crust.

VARIATION

- Drain some tinned plum tomatoes and arrange in a layer in the baking dish before adding the pasta and sauce. Incorporate all of the cheese into the sauce, and scatter 55g (2 oz) of fresh white breadcrumbs over the top to give a crunchy golden topping.
- Use another type of pasta shape such as penne or radiatore.

MUSHROOM AND BACON PASTA

SERVES 4
350g (12 oz) dried pasta shapes
25g (1 oz) butter
2 cloves of garlic
225g (8 oz) mushrooms, sliced
6 rashers bacon, grilled until crisp, chopped
200ml carton single cream
Salt and freshly ground black pepper
2 tbsp chopped, fresh parsley

Cook the pasta shapes according to the packet instructions, drain, leaving a small amount of cooking liquid in the pan.

HOTPLATE
Meanwhile, melt the butter in a pan and gently fry off the garlic then add the mushrooms and cook. Add the bacon and cream, season. Reheat and add the parsley.

Pour the mushroom and bacon sauce into the pasta, quickly mix together and serve at once.

VARIATION
- Substitute the bacon for cooked, diced ham.
- Substitute the bacon for cooked chicken.

SPINACH AND RICOTTA CANNELLONI ⓥ

If you can't get the small cannelloni tubes (from pasta specialists or a good Deli) use 8 longer ones instead. Mustard really helps to bring out the flavour of the cheese.

SERVES 4
Filling
25g (1 oz) butter
1 onion, finely chopped
1 clove of garlic, crushed
350g (12 oz) cooked spinach, chopped
Freshly grated nutmeg
Salt and black pepper
225g (8 oz) Ricotta or curd cheese
25g (1 oz) Parmesan cheese, grated
1 egg, beaten
Pasta, etc.
16 cannelloni tubes, 4cm (1^1/$_2$ inch) in length
600ml (1 pint) béchamel or Foundation White Sauce
  (see p.93)
55g (2 oz) mature Cheddar cheese, grated
1 tsp mustard
Salt and black pepper
Topping
25g (1 oz) mature Cheddar cheese, grated
2 tbsp Parmesan cheese, grated

Melt the butter in a pan and gently fry the onion and garlic until soft but not coloured, mix with the spinach, nutmeg, seasonings, cheeses and egg. Divide the mixture between the cannelloni tubes and place them in a rectangular dish.

Mix the sauce with the cheese, mustard and seasoning. Pour over the cannelloni and sprinkle over the topping cheeses.

MAIN OVEN 190°C (375°F), GAS MARK 5
Place the dish in the centre of the oven and cook for about 30 minutes or until the pasta is cooked and the topping is golden brown.

TIP! This dish can be made in advance, refrigerated and cooked when required.

VARIATION
Rather than a cheese sauce, try a simple tomato based one using 2 cans of chopped tomatoes with onions or peppers, or use a jar of passata.

NOISETTES OF LAMB IN BLACKCURRANT SAUCE

French for hazelnuts, these noisettes are a quick and flavoursome main dish. If the noisettes are very small, buy two per person.

SERVES 4
4 noisettes of lamb
25g (1 oz) butter
1 tbsp olive oil
2 cloves garlic, crushed
Sauce
115g (4 oz) blackcurrant conserve
150ml (^{1}/$_4$ pint) port
Salt and freshly ground black pepper
1 tsp mustard
Grated zest and juice of 1 orange

First make the sauce: Mix the conserve and port together in a saucepan, gently bring to the boil and add the seasoning, mustard, orange zest and juice. Simmer for 5 minutes then strain.

Reduce the strained sauce until thickened and syrupy, to approximately half the amount you started with.

Wipe the lamb with kitchen paper. Melt the butter and oil together in a cast-iron fry pan and gently fry the garlic for a minute.

HOTPLATE
Place the frying pan onto the hottest side of the hotplate and add the lamb noisettes, cook for about 4 minutes either side. The degree of 'doneness' depends upon the thickness and how pink you like your lamb.

Alternatively, if the Main Oven is already hot you can finish cooking the lamb here; after browning both sides of the lamb just transfer the frying pan to the floor of the oven.

Serve at once with a little of the sauce spooned over each noisette. Accompany with mashed potatoes, green beans and roasted squash.

TIP! To roast the squash: prepare and cut into cubes and roast with red pepper and a little olive oil at the top of a hot Main Oven.

MUSHROOM RISOTTO

There are three different ways to cook this risotto! Choose whichever fits into your planning. The hotplate method requires constant stirring and is the traditional method, whereas the oven methods look after themselves.

SERVES 4
25g (1 oz) butter
1 tbsp olive oil
1 onion, chopped
1 clove of garlic, chopped
1 red pepper, diced
225g (8 oz) mixed mushrooms
225g (8 oz) Arborio rice
Salt and freshly ground black pepper
425ml ($^3/_4$ pint) stock
150ml ($^1/_4$ pint) white wine
1 tbsp chopped, fresh parsley
55g (2 oz) Parmesan, grated
2 tbsp cream
Garnish
Shavings of Parmesan cheese

Melt the butter and oil together and sauté the onion, garlic and pepper. Add the mushrooms then the rice. Stir the mixture to coat the rice, season.

HOTPLATE
Gradually pour in the stock and wine, stirring well after each addition.
MAIN OVEN 140°C (275°F) GAS MARK 1
ⓒ LOWER OVEN IN SLOW COOKING MODE
Pour in all the wine and stock at once and bring to the boil, stir and cover. Place the casserole or saucepan into the oven and cook for 20 minutes.

Stir in the parsley at the end of the cooking time, followed by the grated Parmesan and cream. Serve piping hot garnished with shavings of Parmesan.

VARIATIONS
• For Asparagus and Prawn Risotto, substitute the mushrooms for 225g (8 oz) asparagus and add 225g (8 oz) cooked prawns at the end of cooking and heat through.
• For Chicken and Mushroom Risotto add 350g (12 oz) cubed raw chicken fillet and fry off with the mushrooms and continue as above.

POLENTA

Polenta is a ground cornmeal and is generally found as 'quick cook'. It is used in Italian cooking and can be served plain, or mixed with cheese and butter. Polenta is a 'filling' food and may be substituted for rice or potatoes. It is served as a base for many Mediterranean sauces such as a tomato and artichoke heart sauce, chicken livers, or kidneys in red wine. It can even be toasted when cold.

POLENTA WITH SAGE AND EMMENTAL

SERVES 2-3
1 cup of quick cook polenta
Boiling water
1 tbsp fresh sage, chopped
Salt and freshly ground black pepper
3 plum tomatoes, sliced
6 slices of prosciutto
Fresh sage leaves, chopped
Slices of Emmental cheese

Make up the polenta according to the packet instructions and whisk in the chopped sage with the boiling water. Season. Whisk the polenta and when it is very thick place in the base of an ovenproof dish.

Top with the tomato and prosciutto slices. Scatter over a few fresh sage leaves and top with slices of cheese.

MAIN OVEN 200°C (400°F), GAS MARK 6
Cook on the second set of runners until the cheese has melted and the polenta has heated through, about 15 minutes.

Right
Asparagus and Prawn Risotto

SALMON AND DILL SUMMER FLAN

SERVES 6
350g (12 oz) fresh salmon, cooked
225g (8 oz) medium fat curd cheese
225g (8 oz) yoghurt
55g (2 oz) fresh dill, chopped
Grated zest of 1 lemon
2 large eggs
Salt and freshly ground black pepper
25g (1 oz) butter
1 tbsp olive oil
8 sheets of filo pastry
Garnish
Sprig of dill

Flake the cooked salmon, removing any skin and bones. Place the curd cheese, yoghurt, dill, lemon zest and eggs into a large basin and mix well together. Add the flaked fish and season to taste.

Melt the butter with the olive oil. Use 5-6 sheets of the pastry to line a 20cm (8 inch) flan dish or tin, brushing well with the melted butter and oil between each layer of pastry. Let the pastry overhang the sides of the flan dish. Pour the salmon and dill mixture into the pastry case.

Take the remaining filo pastry, roll up and cut into slices. Fold the overhanging pastry to come over the top of the flan dish and arrange the filo pastry loosely over the top of the flan, brush with the remaining butter and oil.

MAIN OVEN 200°C (400°F), GAS MARK 6
Place the flan dish on the floor of the Main Oven and cook for about 25 minutes until browned and the filling has set.

SPINACH AND CHEESE PASTIES

MAKES 6-8
350g (12 oz) cooked spinach, chopped and well drained
55g (2 oz) cooked ham, diced
85g (3 oz) Emmental cheese, grated
Pinch grated nutmeg
1 egg, beaten
Salt and freshly ground black pepper
350g (12 oz) puff pastry
Glaze
Beaten egg

Mix the spinach, ham, cheese, nutmeg and egg together, season. Roll out the pastry and cut into 10cm (4 inch) circles, then roll each circle across the centre to form an oval shape, brush the edges with water. Divide the filling between the pastry ovals and fold over the pastry to form a pasty shape. Seal the edges well. Place on a baking sheet, lined with Bake-O-Glide, brush with the beaten egg glaze.

MAIN OVEN 220°C (425°F), GAS MARK 7
Bake on the second or third set of runners, turning the baking sheet once to ensure even browning, for about 15 minutes until golden brown. Serve warm.

TIP! Shortcrust pastry could be used instead of puff.

SUMMERTIME TOMATO AND EGG BAKE Ⓥ

SERVES 4
900g (2 lb) ripe tomatoes
3 cloves of garlic, sliced
3 tbsp olive oil
4 eggs
2 tbsp parsley, chopped
Salt and freshly ground black pepper

Cut the tomatoes into quarters and remove the cores. Spread over a 1.5 litre (2¾ pint) shallow ovenproof dish. Sprinkle the garlic over the tomatoes and drizzle with the olive oil. Season well and stir together.

MAIN OVEN 200°C (400°F), GAS MARK 6
Place the dish in the centre of the oven and bake for about 40 minutes, or until the tomatoes have softened. Remove from the oven and make four gaps within the tomatoes, break an egg into each gap and return to the oven for 5-10 minutes, until the eggs are cooked to your liking.

Scatter over the parsley and serve at once with chunks of fresh bread.

SWEET AND SOUR PORK

SERVES 2-3
225g (8 oz) pork fillet or tenderloin
1 tsp oil
2.5cm (¹/₂ inch) root ginger, peeled and grated
1 bunch spring onions, sliced
1 small red pepper, seeded and chopped
225g (8 oz) can pineapple pieces, in natural juice
Sauce
2 tbsp tomato ketchup
2 tbsp dark soy sauce
1 tbsp malt vinegar
1 tbsp clear honey
2 tsp cornflour

Cut the pork into thin strips. Heat the oil in a large saucepan on the hotplate. Add the pork and ginger and cook until browning. Add the onions and pepper, stir-fry for 2-3 minutes. Drain the pineapple and reserve the juice. Add the pineapple pieces to the pork.

In a basin, mix the sauce ingredients together with the reserved pineapple juice. Pour over the pork and stir until the sauce has thickened. Serve over a bed of steamed rice.

TANDOORI CHICKEN WITH MINT YOGHURT

SERVES 4
2 packets mini chicken fillets, or 3-4 chicken breasts cut into 2.5cm (1 inch) strips
Juice of ¹/₂ lemon
¹/₂ tsp salt
¹/₄ tsp cardamom seeds
2 tsp cumin seeds
1 tsp fennel seeds
3 tsp fresh ginger, grated
2 cloves of garlic, crushed
1 tsp chilli powder
200g tub of natural yoghurt
Mint yoghurt
200g Greek yoghurt
1 tbsp chopped, fresh mint,
¹/₄ tsp salt
1 tsp caster sugar

Place the chicken fillets in a basin and squeeze over the lemon juice and sprinkle with the salt. Mix well together.

Heat a small frying pan and dry-fry the cardamom, cumin and fennel seeds for 2 minutes until the seeds begin to colour. Transfer to a large bowl and add the ginger, garlic, chilli powder and yoghurt and mix together. Stir in the chicken fillets and chill overnight.

MAIN OVEN 230°C (450°F), GAS MARK 8
Place the chicken on the grill rack set in the Rayburn meat tin and slide onto the top set of runners. Grill for about 15-20 minutes, until cooked.

Meanwhile, make the Mint Yoghurt: mix the yoghurt, mint, salt and sugar together. Serve the chicken with the Mint Yoghurt.

TOMATO AND OLIVE TARTE TATIN ⓥ

Use a cast-iron or non-stick cast-aluminium frying pan with a detachable handle so that hotplate and oven cooking can take place in the same pan.

SERVES 4
2 tbsp olive oil
1 tsp caster sugar
8 tomatoes
Black olives, pitted
Salt and freshly ground black pepper
Topping
115g (4 oz) plain flour
55g (2 oz) butter
55g (2 oz) mature Cheddar cheese, grated
2 tsp chives, chopped
Freshly ground black pepper
Water

Place the olive oil in the base of a cast-iron frying pan with the sugar. Heat until the sugar begins to caramelise. Cut the tomatoes in half horizontally and add to the oil (cut side down) packing them well into the pan. Heat, until the tomatoes are beginning to soften, about 4-5 minutes. Season. Arrange the black olives around the tomatoes.

Meanwhile make the topping: place the flour, butter, cheese and chives into a food processor and process until the mixture resembles breadcrumbs. Season. Add enough water to form dough. Roll out into a circle slightly larger then the pan. Place over the tomatoes, tucking the edges down the sides. Place the pan into the oven and remove the handle.

MAIN OVEN 220°C (425°F), GAS MARK 7
Cook on the second or third runners down for 15-20 minutes, until golden brown.

Let the Tarte Tatin cool for a few minutes, then turn out and garnish.

VEGETABLE AND SAUSAGE FRITTATA

SERVES 3-4
2 tbsp olive oil
115g (4 oz) sliced, spicy sausage, such as chorizo
115g (4 oz) mushrooms, sliced
1 red pepper, chopped
115g (4 oz) new potatoes, cooked and cubed
1 small red onion
6 eggs
115g (4 oz) cheese, grated
Parsley
Salt and freshly ground black pepper

Heat the olive oil in a cast-iron omelette pan or 24cm (9½ inch) non-stick cast aluminium frying pan and sauté the sausage, mushrooms, pepper, potatoes and onion until all are heated through and cooked.

Beat the eggs with the cheese and parsley, season to taste. Pour into the pan and cook quickly for 3-4 minutes on the hotplate then move to the top of the oven to finish cooking.

MAIN OVEN 220°C (425°F), GAS MARK 7
Cook at the top of the oven, for about 4-6 minutes, or until the egg has set.

Slide onto a serving dish and cut into wedges to serve.

Right
Vegetable Frittata

SAUCES AND ACCOMPANIMENTS

In this chapter we have included a good range of sauces and accompaniments useful to the busy cook. Many are formed from a basic recipe that can then be varied. Take time to select a sauce that can, if needed, add colour and complement the food, but does not compete with the main flavours. Finished sauces can be made ahead to minimise last minute preparations.

APPLE SAUCE

SERVES 4
450g (1 lb) cooking apples
4 tbsp water
A thinly pared piece of lemon zest
25g (1 oz) butter
Caster sugar to taste

Wipe the apples but do not peel or core. Cut into rough chunks and place in a pan with the water and lemon zest. Cover and place the pan on the simmering end of the hotplate for 5 minutes. Remove the lid and give the contents a good stir.

MAIN OVEN 120°C (250°F), GAS MARK L-1
© LOWER OVEN IN SLOW COOKING MODE
Replace the lid and transfer the pan to the floor of the oven for 20-30 minutes, until the apple has turned to a pulp. Remove from the oven and allow to cool. Pass the pulp through a nylon sieve and return to the rinsed pan. Stir in the butter and sugar but avoid over-sweetening the sauce – it should provide a good contrast to cut through the richness of meats such as pork.

BREAD SAUCE

SERVES 4
1 small onion
2 cloves
1 bay leaf
300ml (10 fl oz) milk
115g (4 oz) fresh white breadcrumbs
Salt and freshly ground black pepper
2-3 gratings of a fresh nutmeg
25g (1 oz) butter
A little double cream

Stud the onion with the cloves and place with the bay leaf and milk in a small pan. Scald the milk on the simmering end of the hotplate and then cover. Leave the pan at the back of the top plate for at least an hour to allow the milk to infuse. Remove the bay leaf and onion and add the breadcrumbs and butter. Season to taste and add the cream just before serving. Add extra milk or breadcrumbs if you feel the sauce is too thick or thin.

CHILLI JAM

MAKES 1 X 450G (1 LB) JAR
This jam is excellent with poultry and as a dipping condiment to serve with seafood. It's also very good smeared on chicken thighs before roasting in a hot oven.

4 plump cloves of garlic
2 red peppers
10 red chillies
1 tbsp olive oil
55g (2 oz) demerara sugar
3 tbsp red wine vinegar
1 x 400g can of Italian tomatoes
Salt and freshly ground black pepper

Peel the garlic, de-seed the peppers and chillies and slice thinly. Lightly sweat in the oil for 10-12 minutes in a pan on the simmering end of the hotplate. Add the sugar and when dissolved, add the vinegar. Finally, add the tomatoes and cover. Simmer gently for 15 minutes until it has a jammy consistency. Allow to cool a little then season to taste and process in a blender. If you prefer a totally smooth consistency, pass it through a nylon sieve. Can be stored in a clean glass jar in the refrigerator for up to a week.

FOUNDATION WHITE SAUCE

SERVES 4
25g (1 oz) butter
25g (1 oz) plain flour
300ml (10 fl oz) milk
Seasoning

Melt the butter in a small saucepan on the simmering end of the hotplate. Stir in the flour and cook for a minute or two, stirring. Take the pan off the heat and gradually blend in the milk. If the milk is warm it will be absorbed more quickly. Therefore, it's a good idea to put a measuring jug of milk to warm on the top of the cooker or in the Lower Oven for a short time, depending on setting. Once all the milk has been absorbed, if the sauce is not to have a further period of cooking (e.g. in the oven in an assembled dish such as in a lasagne topping) it is important that the sauce continues to cook slowly for a few minutes to avoid a raw flour taste.

VARIATIONS

CHEESE SAUCE

Use a mixture of Gruyère and Parmesan cheese and add a little English mustard to give definition.

FISH SAUCE

Use a proportion of poaching liquid with the milk for extra flavour, plus add a few drops of anchovy essence (optional).

ONION SAUCE

Soften a large chopped onion in stock before adding to the thickened sauce, season well with white pepper.

MUSTARD SAUCE

Add 1 tsp of English mustard powder and a few drops of white wine vinegar.

PARSLEY SAUCE

Add fresh chopped parsley just before serving, with a few drops of lemon juice.

PRAWN SAUCE

Add some chopped prawns a couple of minutes before serving, so that they heat through without deteriorating. Reserve some whole prawns for garnishing each portion.

GOOSEBERRY SAUCE

SERVES 4

350g (12 oz) gooseberries, topped and tailed
30ml (1 fl oz) water
25g (1 oz) butter
25g (1 oz) caster sugar
Zest and juice of $^{1}/_{2}$ an orange
Salt and white pepper

Place the gooseberries and water in a small pan, cover and simmer for 5 minutes, until tender. Pass the fruit through a nylon sieve. Return them to the rinsed pan with the other ingredients and adjust the seasoning. Serve with mackerel, herrings, sprats or roast duck.

HOLLANDAISE SAUCE

SERVES 4

175g (6 oz) butter
2 tbsp lemon juice
1 tbsp white wine vinegar
6 large egg yolks
1 tsp caster sugar
A pinch of salt

Place the butter in a small pan and the lemon juice and vinegar in another. Set both to heat on the simmering end of the hotplate until the butter is melted and hot and the other pan is starting to bubble. Fill a liquidiser goblet or food processor bowl complete with blade with very hot but not boiling water and leave for a minute, and pour away.

Add the yolks, sugar and salt and process for just a few seconds. Pour the lemon juice and vinegar mixture into a jug and pour in a thin stream, slowly onto the yolks, with the machine running. Immediately, pour the foaming butter into the jug and pour this slowly onto the egg mixture. Transfer the finished Hollandaise into the jug and keep warm on a cloth on the top plate until it is needed.

TIP! The ingredients can be halved if necessary.

VARIATION
BEARNAISE SAUCE

Follow the Hollandaise recipe replacing the white wine vinegar with tarragon vinegar and finish with plenty of finely chopped fresh tarragon.

HOMEMADE GRAVY

SERVES 4

2 tbsp fat from meat tin
2 tbsp plain flour for thin gravy or 4 tbsp plain flour for thick gravy
300ml (10 fl oz) meat stock or vegetable water

Transfer your meat or poultry to a warmed dish to keep hot in the Lower Oven or next to the Rayburn before carving. Pour most of the fat from the meat tin into a bowl leaving 2 tbsp of fat in the meat tin with the meat juices and the caramelised deposits from roasting. Place the tin directly on the simmering end of the

hotplate and stir the flour into the fat. Cook for a few minutes, using a flat-ended wooden spatula. Gradually add the stock until well blended. Allow to come to the boil and simmer for several minutes until thickened. Adjust the consistency to taste and season well.
If you roast a few peeled vegetables such as carrots and onions to the meat tin whilst roasting, they will help to add flavour and colour to the gravy.

SPICED CRANBERRY SAUCE WITH PORT

SERVES 4
140g (5 oz) granulated sugar
225ml (8 fl oz) orange juice
225g (8 oz) fresh cranberries
1 tsp ground allspice
1 tsp arrowroot
2 tbsp port

Dissolve the sugar in the orange juice in a pan on the simmering end of the hotplate and then add the cranberries and spice. Cover and bring just to the boil.

© LOWER OVEN IN SLOW COOKING MODE
Continue to cook very slowly until the berries are tender, about 10-15 minutes. Mix the arrowroot in a little cold water and stir into the sauce, cook for a minute on the simmering end of the hotplate until slightly thickened and glossy. Cool and stir in the port before storing in the refrigerator.

CHESTNUT STUFFING

SUFFICIENT FOR A 3.6-4.5 KG (8-10 LB) TURKEY
450g (1 lb) chestnuts
300ml (10 fl oz) stock
55g (2 oz) butter
Salt and freshly ground black pepper
Nutmeg, freshly grated

Slit the chestnuts with a sharp knife and roast in the oven or boil for 10 minutes on the hotplate. Using a small paring knife, peel away the inner and outer skins. Place the chestnuts in a pan with the stock and bring to the boil and then simmer for 25-30 minutes. Allow to cool, once cooled, purée: using either a food processor or pass through a sieve. Work in the butter and seasoning. Use for stuffing roast turkey.

PARSLEY AND THYME STUFFING

SUFFICIENT FOR A 1.5-1.75 KG (3-4 LB) CHICKEN
25g (1 oz) butter
1 medium onion, peeled and finely chopped
450g (1 lb) good quality pork sausages
175g (6 oz) fresh white breadcrumbs
6 tbsp freshly chopped parsley
2 tsp freshly chopped thyme
1/2 tsp Marigold Swiss vegetable bouillon powder
Salt and freshly ground black pepper
1 large egg

Melt the butter in a pan and add the onion. Fry until soft and then take off the heat and allow to go cold. Slit the sausages with a sharp knife and remove the sausage meat. Add to the onion with the other ingredients, and mix thoroughly. If it seems a little dry, add a little milk to give a soft consistency.

SAGE AND ONION STUFFING

SUFFICIENT FOR A 3.6-4.5 KG (8-10 LB) GOOSE
900g (2 lbs) onions
25g (1 oz) butter
Salt and freshly ground black pepper
2-3 tsp dried sage
125-175g (4-6 oz) fresh white breadcrumbs

Skin and roughly chop the onions. Cook in a little water for 15-20 minutes, until just tender, drain well, reserving the water for gravy. Mash the onions to a pulp with a potato masher, add the butter, sage and seasoning, work in enough breadcrumbs to make a soft stuffing.

VARIATION
Use half this quantity when cooking and stuffing a duck.

BRANDY SAUCE

SERVES 4
300 ml (10 fl oz) Foundation White Sauce (see p93),
  seasoning omitted
2 tbsp brandy, to taste
2 tbsp caster sugar

Add the brandy and sugar to the finished white sauce.
Serve with Christmas Pudding.

JAM SAUCE

SERVES 4
6 tbsp jam
150ml (5 fl oz) water
A few drops of lemon juice
1 tsp arrowroot

Place the jam, water and lemon juice in a small pan
and heat gently on the simmering end of the hotplate.
In a cup mix the arrowroot with a little cold water.
With the pan off the heat, whisk in the arrowroot.
Return to the simmering end of the hotplate and cook
gently, stirring, until the sauce is clear. If necessary, add
a little extra water to thin further. Taste to check the
balance and lemon juice level. Serve with steamed
and baked puddings and banana fritters.

CUSTARD SAUCE

SERVES 4
600ml (1 pint) milk
1 tbsp cornflour
2 eggs
55g (2 oz) caster sugar
1/2 tsp vanilla extract

Blend a little of the cold milk with the cornflour in a
small basin. Heat the rest of the milk in a pan on the
simmering end of the hotplate. When the milk begins
to steam, take off the heat and whisk in the cornflour.
Cook for 2 minutes, stirring. Break the eggs into a bowl
and whisk in the sugar. Take the pan off the heat and
whisk in the eggs and sugar. Return the pan to the
simmering end and stir until the sauce thickens, do not
boil. Add the vanilla extract. If vanilla sugar is available,
this may be used in place of the caster sugar and extract.

GINGER SAUCE

SERVES 4
6 slices of stem ginger, chopped finely
3 tbsp ginger syrup from the stem ginger
8 tbsp apple juice
2 tbsp caster sugar
Juice of half a lemon

Place all the ingredients in a small pan and heat gently
on the simmering end of the hotplate until the sugar
has dissolved. Taste and adjust the sugar and lemon
juice levels. Serve with steamed and baked puddings.

CHOCOLATE SAUCE

SERVES 4
175g (6 oz) good quality plain chocolate
175ml (6 fl oz) water
115g (4 oz) caster sugar
55g (2 oz) butter
1 tsp vanilla extract

Place all the ingredients in a small pan, heat gently on
the simmering end of the hotplate, stirring occasionally
until melted. Serve hot with Chocolate Sponge Pudding
(*see* p109) or Profiteroles (*see* p111)

STICKY TOFFEE SAUCE

SERVES 4
115g (4 oz) butter
175g (6 oz) soft brown sugar
150ml (5 fl oz) double cream
1 tsp vanilla extract

Melt the butter, sugar and cream in a small pan on the
simmering end of the hotplate. Once the butter has
melted and the sugar dissolved, bring to a gentle simmer
for a few minutes. Cool a little before adding the vanilla.
Use to line the base of a sponge pudding or as an
ingredient for other desserts. To serve with Sticky Toffee
Pudding (*see* p114), add a little boiling water to thin to a
suitable consistency before pouring over the pudding.

PUDDINGS AND DESSERTS

It's easy to produce an array of delicious puddings and desserts with your Rayburn. From family favourites such as fruit crumble to fancier creations like Profiteroles, these can all be created with confidence. We have also included a number of recipes that can be slow-cooked using the Main Oven when it is at an idling setting between meals.

APRICOT FLAN

SERVES 8
Although this recipe calls for canned fruit, do use ripe fresh apricots if you have them.

Pastry
225g (8 oz) plain flour
2 tbsp icing sugar
115g (4 oz) butter
3-4 tbsp cold water
Filling
85g (3 oz) butter
85g (3 oz) caster sugar
1 large egg
A few drops of almond extract
85g (3 oz) ground almonds
2 cans of apricot halves, drained
25g (1 oz) flaked almonds

Make shortcrust pastry in the normal way. Roll out to line a 20cm (8 inch) flan dish and prick with a fork. Cream the butter and sugar together, beat in the egg, then the almond extract and ground almonds. Drain the apricot halves and pat dry with kitchen paper. Arrange over the base of the flan, then spread the frangipane mixture evenly over the top and sprinkle with the flaked almonds.

MAIN OVEN 180°C (350°F), GAS MARK 4
Cook on the floor of the oven for about 25-30 minutes until golden brown. If browning too quickly, slide in a cold plain shelf on the second set of runners above.

BAKED APPLES

SERVES 4
55g (2 oz) butter
4 medium Bramley apples, each approx. 175g (6 oz)
4 tbsp apple juice
115g (4 oz) sultanas
55g (2 oz) pecan nuts, chopped (optional)
6 tbsp maple syrup

Generously butter a shallow ovenproof dish with half the butter. Core the apples and score the skin around the middle of each apple to prevent bursting. Arrange the apples in the dish and add the juice. Divide the sultanas between the centres of the apples, add the nuts if using, and drizzle the maple syrup over each. Place the rest of the butter equally over the tops of the apples.

MAIN OVEN 180°C (350°F), GAS MARK 4
Bake in the middle of the oven for 30-40 minutes until tender, basting twice with the buttery juices. Alternatively, cook at an idling temperature for a much longer period.

BAKED RUM BANANAS

SERVES 4
6 firm bananas
Juice of 1 lemon
3 tbsp Demerara sugar
3 tbsp water
100ml (3$\frac{1}{2}$ fl oz) rum
To serve
Cream or crème fraîche

Peel the bananas and cut each one into 4 chunks. Place in an ovenproof dish and pour over the lemon juice. Sprinkle over the sugar and water.

MAIN OVEN 220°C (425°F), GAS MARK 7
Cook on the second or third runners until lightly browned. Turn the bananas over and add the rum and cook for another 10 minutes.

Transfer the bananas to a warmed dish and place in the Lower Oven to keep warm. Reduce the rum sauce by boiling rapidly, until it thickens slightly. Pour over the bananas and serve with dollops of cream or crème fraîche.

BAKED CUSTARD

SERVES 4-6
25g (1 oz) butter
600ml (1 pint) full-cream milk
3 large eggs, beaten
25g (1 oz) caster sugar
Freshly grated nutmeg

Generously butter a 850ml (1$\frac{1}{2}$ pint) pie dish. In a pan, heat the milk on the simmering end of the hotplate until steaming, remove from the heat and whisk in the eggs and sugar.

Right
Apricot Flan

Strain into the pie dish and grate some nutmeg over the top.

MAIN OVEN 150°C (300°F), GAS MARK 2
Stand in a meat tin half filled with boiling water. Lightly cover with foil and hang on the lowest set of runners and slide a cold plain shelf in above. Cook for 1-1$\frac{1}{2}$ hours until the custard is just set, it will become firmer after being chilled. Alternatively, cook on the floor of the oven at an idling temperature for a longer period.

BAKEWELL PUDDING

SERVES 4-6
As well as serving this as a delicious pudding at the end of a meal, it can also be served as a pastry. Sweet and savoury pastry cases are worth making and freezing raw, as they can then be quickly turned into a recipe such as this.

Pastry
175g (6 oz) plain flour
1 tbsp icing sugar
40g (1$\frac{1}{2}$ oz) butter
40g (1$\frac{1}{2}$ oz) vegetable shortening
2-3 tbsp cold water
Filling
5 tbsp jam – raspberry, strawberry or apricot
115g (4 oz) butter
3 large eggs, beaten
85g (3 oz) caster sugar
85g (3 oz) ground almonds
$\frac{1}{2}$ tsp almond extract
25g (1 oz) flaked almonds

For the filling, loosen the lid of the jar of jam and place next to a small bowl containing the butter on the warm top plate while you make the pastry. To make the pastry, sift the flour into a mixing bowl, then add the icing sugar and cut the fat into small dice and rub into the flour. Add just enough water to form a firm dough. Turn out and pat into a flattened disk shape, wrap in clingfilm and chill for 30 minutes. Roll out and line a 20cm (8 inch) deep pie dish or flan case. Spread the jam evenly over the pastry. Beat the eggs and sugar until light and fluffy, then stir in the melted butter, ground almonds and extract and pour over the jam. Sprinkle over the flaked almonds.

MAIN OVEN 200°C (400°F), GAS MARK 6
Place the dish on the floor of the oven to bake for 25-30 minutes, or until the filling has set. Slide a cold plain shelf on the second set of runners above if browning too quickly. Dust the edge of the tart with a little sieved icing sugar and serve with Custard Sauce (*see* p96).

VARIATIONS
225-350g (8-12 oz) fresh raspberries or other berry fruits can be added before the frangipane mixture is added. If preferred, omit the flaked almonds and ice the baked pie with a thin layer of simple glacé icing, using: 115g (4 oz) sieved icing sugar and 1-2 tbsp sieved lemon juice. Decorate with halved glacé cherries (this is also known as Trentham Tart).

BLUE MOUNTAIN PIE

SERVES 10-12
This is an upmarket version of the original recipe, it's less well known than its more famous, but rather sickly, relation Banoffi Pie. The beauty of this pie is that the coffee cream doesn't make it too sweet. The cooked cans of caramel can be made in batches ahead of time when the cooker is idling – they last for at least 6 months, but be sure to date the tin.

Caramel
1 x 400g can sweetened condensed milk
Pastry
175g (6 oz) plain flour
1 tbsp icing sugar
85g (3 oz) butter
2-3 tbsp cold water
Topping
3 large firm bananas
2-3 tbsp Tia Maria or Kahlúa
426ml (15 fl oz) double cream
1-2 tbsp icing sugar
2-3 tbsp Camp coffee essence

To make the caramel, place the unopened can of condensed milk in a deep saucepan and pour over boiling water to cover by 2.5cm (1 inch). Bring to the boil, cover and keep slowly simmering on the hotplate for 30 minutes.

MAIN OVEN 120°C (250°F), GAS MARK L-1
Ⓒ LOWER OVEN IN SLOW COOKING MODE
Transfer the pan to the floor of the oven for a further 2 hours. Remove the pan from the oven, drain off the water and then pour over enough cold water to cover

the can. Leave until the can is just warm, ready for use.

Sieve the flour into a mixing bowl, stir in the sugar and cut the butter into dice and rub into the flour or process lightly in a food processor. Add just enough water so that the mixture just starts to cohere. Roll out on a floured board and use to line a 23cm (9 inch) loose-based fluted flan tin. Prick the base with a fork and freeze for an hour.

MAIN OVEN 200°C (400°F), GAS MARK 6
Bake on the floor of the oven for 10-15 minutes, until a very pale golden colour, turning once during cooking. Allow to cool completely.

Warm the unopened caramel can on the top plate for 30 minutes before using so that is becomes easy to spread. Carefully open the can and spread the warm caramel across the base of the pastry case and chill. Slice over the bananas, and sprinkle with the coffee liqueur.

Sieve the icing sugar into the cream and add the coffee essence – the finished topping needs to be a light coffee colour. Whip until it just holds its shape. Pile or pipe onto the bananas and chill. Best served the day after making.

BREAD AND BUTTER PUDDING

SERVES 4-6
55g (2 oz) soft butter
8-10 medium slices of white bread
115g (4 oz) sultanas
3 large eggs
55g (2 oz) caster sugar
Zest of 1 lemon
600ml (1 pint) milk
1 vanilla pod
2 tbsp demerara sugar
To decorate:
A little sieved apricot jam or a little sieved icing sugar

Generously butter a 1.7 litre (3 pint) ovenproof dish. Lightly butter the bread and remove the crusts. Cut into rectangles or triangles and arrange in the dish, layering with the sultanas, but don't leave any sultanas on the top of the pudding or they will become hard and taste burnt.

In a mixing bowl, whisk the eggs with the sugar and lemon zest. On the hotplate, bring the milk just to boiling point. Split the vanilla pod and scrape out the seeds using the back of a sharp knife, add the two halves and seeds to the milk. Transfer the pan onto the top plate for 10 minutes, to allow the milk to stay hot and infuse with the vanilla. Remove the two pod halves and pour the milk over the eggs and sugar, stirring well. Pour this mixture over the bread and butter and leave to stand for 30 minutes before cooking.

MAIN OVEN 180°C (350°F), GAS MARK 4
Sprinkle with the demerara sugar before baking in the centre of the oven for 45-50 minutes, until risen and golden brown. Warm the sieved apricot jam and brush over the top before serving, or alternatively dust with a little icing sugar. Serve warm.

VARIATIONS
• Use briôche, croissants or teacakes.
• Sandwich with marmalade, ginger preserve or lemon curd before placing into the dish.
• Alternatively, consider adding 4 tbsp whisky or rum to the custard, or soak the sultanas in a little brandy.

BREAD PUDDING

SERVES 8-10
450g (1 lb) leftover bread, buns, etc.
85g (3 oz) shredded suet
115g (4 oz) caster sugar
115g (4 oz) sultanas
115g (4 oz) currants
2 tsp ground mixed spice
2 large eggs, beaten
2 tbsp maple or golden syrup
2 tbsp black treacle
A little caster sugar to sprinkle on top

Tear or cut the bread up into rough chunks, leaving the crusts on. Place in a mixing bowl and cover with cold water, leave to stand for 2 hours. Drain in a colander and squeeze out as much water as possible. Return to the bowl and break up with a fork. Add the suet, sugar, fruit, spice, eggs, syrup and treacle. Mix thoroughly and then turn into a buttered 26 x 18cm (10$\frac{1}{2}$ x 7 inch) 5cm (2 inch) deep tin. Smooth the surface and sprinkle with a little extra caster sugar.

MAIN OVEN 190°C (375°F), GAS MARK 5
Bake in the centre of the oven for about an hour or until

set. This is a forgiving recipe and may be cooked for a much longer time in a cooler oven. Serve warm, cut into squares.

HOT CHOCOLATE SOUFFLES

SERVES 6
4 tbsp double cream
$1/2$ orange, juice and finely grated zest
225g (8 oz) good quality plain chocolate, finely chopped
85g (3 oz) caster sugar
$1/2$ tsp vanilla extract
4 large egg yolks
6 large egg whites
A pinch of salt
Icing sugar, for dusting
To prepare dishes
Unsalted butter
Caster sugar

Butter 6 small ovenproof soufflé dishes or large ramekins and dust with caster sugar. Place the cream, orange zest and juice into a medium-sized saucepan, and place on the boiling end of the hotplate. As soon as the cream mixture is almost boiling, add the chocolate and then leave the pan on a cloth on the top plate for 5 minutes. Stir the mixture until the chocolate has melted and become smooth. Remove from the cooker and stir in the sugar and vanilla extract, then the egg yolks, one at a time. Whisk the egg whites with the salt until stiff. Fold a large spoonful of the egg whites into the chocolate sauce to slacken it, continue to fold in the remainder. Pour into the prepared soufflé dishes, then bake immediately, or freeze at this point until wanted (wrapped tightly in cling film).

MAIN OVEN 200°C (400°F), GAS MARK 6
Bake on a baking tray on a grid shelf on the third set of runners down. Cook for 15-20 minutes, or 20-25 minutes if cooking straight from the freezer, until well risen. Lightly dust with a little icing sugar and serve at once with pistachio ice cream.

CHOCOLATE TART

SERVES 8
Unlike many versions of chocolate tart which can be rather heavy and cloying, this tart has a relatively light filling which contrasts well with the crisp buttery pastry below.

Pastry
225g (8 oz) plain flour
2 tbsp icing sugar
115g (4 oz) butter
3-4 tbsp cold water
Filling
3 medium eggs
1 medium egg yolk
115g (4 oz) caster sugar
350g (12 oz) good quality plain chocolate
55g (2 oz) unsalted butter
30ml (1 fl oz) double cream
50ml (2 fl oz) brandy

Sift the flour into a mixing bowl and stir in the icing sugar. Cut the butter into dice and rub into the flour, or process lightly in a food processor. Add just enough water so that the mixture just starts to cohere. Roll out on a floured board and use to line a 23cm (9 inch) loose-based fluted flan tin. Prick the base with a fork and freeze for an hour.

MAIN OVEN 190°C (375°F), GAS MARK 5
Bake on the floor of the oven for 15-25 minutes, until a very pale golden colour, turning once during cooking. Allow to cool completely.

Place the eggs, extra yolk and sugar in a mixing bowl. Place the bowl on a cloth on the top plate for 30-40 minutes until the ingredients have become warm. At the same time, place the chocolate, butter, cream and brandy in a smaller bowl to melt in the same way. Whisk together the egg and sugar mixture until it becomes pale and doubles in volume. Carefully fold the chocolate mixture into the egg and stir to blend. Pour this into the cooked pastry case and bake on a grid shelf on the lowest set of runners for about 12-15 minutes, until set. Leave to become quite cool to set before taking out of the tin.

Right
Hot Chocolate Souffle

CHRISTMAS PUDDING

Steaming the puddings in the oven saves you the bother of having to endlessly check on the cooking, and dispenses with any need for topping up with hot water. The kitchen can remain steam-free too, as with all oven steamed recipes.

MAKES 2 X 750G (1$^1/_2$ LB) PUDDINGS
175g (6 oz) seedless raisins
175g (6 oz) stoned prunes, chopped
175g (6 oz) shredded suet
175g (6 oz) soft brown sugar
175g (6 oz) self raising flour
115g (4 oz) chopped mixed peel
Grated zest of 1 orange
55g (2 oz) glacé cherries, quartered
1 tsp mixed spice
$^1/_2$ tsp freshly grated nutmeg
4 large eggs, beaten
150ml (5 fl oz) stout
2 tbsp brandy

Combine all the dry ingredients in a mixing bowl and mix in the beaten eggs. When well combined, add the stout and brandy and mix again thoroughly. Pile into buttered basins and cover with a pleated disk of both baking parchment and foil and fix securely. Place on a trivet or small enamel plate in a saucepan and pour boiling water to come halfway up the side of the basin. Cover and bring to the boil. Adjust the position on the hotplate to maintain a medium boil for 30 minutes, continue to steam for 1$^1/_2$-2$^1/_2$ hours.

MAIN OVEN 120°C (250°F), GAS MARK L-1
© LOWER OVEN IN SLOW COOKING MODE
Transfer to the floor of the Main Oven, where no topping up will be required. Alternatively, continue steaming on the hotplate, topping up with boiling water as necessary. Allow to cool and store in a cool, dry and dark place for at least a month. To serve, steam for an hour using the above methods.

CLAFOUTIS

SERVES 4-6
450g (1 lb) black cherries
125ml (4 fl oz) full cream milk
150ml (5 fl oz) double cream
$^1/_2$ tsp vanilla extract
4 large eggs

115g (4 oz) caster sugar
25g (1 oz) plain flour
Soft butter for greasing
25g (1 oz) icing sugar

If necessary, drain the cherries, and then stone them. Bring the milk, cream and vanilla extract to the boil, and whisk the eggs and sugar until pale and light. Sift in the flour and whisk again. Generously butter a 25 x 23cm (10 x 9 inch) oval ovenproof dish, approx. 4cm (1$^1/_2$ inches) high and arrange the cherries evenly in the base of the dish. Strain the hot milk into the batter, whisk well and immediately pour over the cherries.

MAIN OVEN 200°C (400°F), GAS MARK 6
Bake near the top of the oven for 20-30 minutes until golden and risen. Remove and serve warm, dredge with the icing sugar just before serving.

VARIATIONS
• Red cherries with crème de cassis
• Fresh apricots on a thin base of apricot jam
• Tinned pear halves dusted with cinnamon
• Diced apples and halved strawberries.

CRUMBLE

SERVES 4-6
Topping
175g (6 oz) self raising flour
85g (3 oz) butter or *margarine*
40-85g (1$^1/_2$-3 oz) demerara sugar
Fruit
675g (1$^1/_2$ lb) prepared fruit
115-140g (4-5 oz) sugar
4 tbsp water or *fruit juice* or *cordial*

Place the fruit in an ovenproof dish and add the sugar and liquid. Rub the topping ingredients together and sprinkle over the fruit.

MAIN OVEN 180°C (350°F), GAS MARK 4
Bake for at least 30 minutes in the centre of the oven, slightly longer for harder fruits. Alternatively, cook on the floor of the oven at an idling temperature for a longer period.

VARIATIONS
The following fruit and topping combinations are particular favourites of ours:

RHUBARB AND GINGER
2 tsp dried ginger in the topping, chopped stem or glacé pieces with the fruit.

RHUBARB AND ORANGE
Use orange juice reduced to a syrupy consistency and add to the fruit.

STRAWBERRY AND GOOSEBERRY
Poach the gooseberries until tender, then add the strawberries and topping and bake.

SUMMER FRUITS
Use Summer Pudding soft fruit mixtures, fresh or frozen.

ALMOND CRUMBLE TOPPING
Replace 25g (1 oz) of the flour with ground almonds.

CARRIBEAN CRUMBLE TOPPING
Replace 55g (2 oz) of the flour with desiccated coconut.

OAT CRUMBLE TOPPING
Replace 55g (2 oz) of the flour with porridge oats.

WHOLEWHEAT CRUMBLE TOPPING
Replace 85g (3 oz) of the white flour with wholemeal.

CREME BRULEE

SERVES 6
Custard
600ml (1 pint) double cream
A strip of lemon zest
4 medium egg yolks
55g (2 oz) caster sugar
1 tsp vanilla extract
A little soft butter
Caramel
175g (6 oz) caster sugar
3 tbsp cold water

Place the cream and lemon zest in a heavy-based pan and place on the boiling end of the hotplate, bring to boiling point, watching carefully. Remove from the heat, cover and leave to infuse for 30 minutes. Whisk the egg yolks, sugar and vanilla together in a mixing bowl. Pour over the hot cream, whisking well and return to the pan, removing the strip of lemon. Now place this pan barely on the simmering end of the hotplate and stir for 2 minutes. Pour into a 850ml (1½ pint) shallow

ovenproof dish or 6 small ramekins, lightly buttered before filling.

MAIN OVEN 150°C (300°F), GAS MARK 2
Place in a meat tin containing enough boiling water to come halfway up the sides. Bake in the middle of the oven for about 60 minutes, until set but still slightly wobbly. Leave to cool, then chill overnight – as they cool they will become firmer.

To make the caramel: place the water and sugar into a heavy-based pan and leave on the simmering end of the hotplate until the sugar dissolves. When this has happened, transfer to the boiling end of the hotplate and boil hard until the mixture starts to resemble the colour of runny honey. Pour slowly and carefully over the custard. Allow to set in the refrigerator and serve the same day. Take care not to splash the caramel as it is very hot. To clean the pan simply boil up some water to dissolve the hardened caramel.

VARIATIONS
Add fruit compôte beneath the custard, such as mango and banana.

CREME CARAMEL

SERVES 6
Caramel
115g (4 oz) granulated sugar
150ml (5 fl oz) water
Custard
4 large eggs
1 large egg yolk
85g (3 oz) caster sugar
1 tsp vanilla extract
600ml (1 pint) milk

Place the sugar in a heavy-based pan and add all but a tablespoon of the water. Place on the simmering end of the hotplate and allow the sugar to dissolve. Then move to the boiling end of the hotplate and boil rapidly until the sugar turns a dark golden colour. Immediately remove from the heat and carefully add the rest of the water to arrest the cooking – it will bubble violently at this point so take care. Pour at once into a lightly oiled 1litre (2 pint) soufflé dish or 6 ramekins, and leave to set. Whisk the eggs with the sugar and vanilla extract in a bowl. Heat the milk on the simmering end of the hotplate until steaming and pour over the eggs, whisking constantly. Strain the custard onto the caramel and allow any bubbles to subside.

MAIN OVEN 150°C (300°F), GAS MARK 2
Stand in a meat tin half filled with boiling water. Lightly cover with foil and hang on the lowest set of runners and slide a cold plain shelf in above. Cook for 1-1$\frac{1}{2}$ hours until the custard is just set, it will become firmer after being chilled. Alternatively, cook on the floor of the oven at an idling temperature for a longer period. Leave in the refrigerator overnight and loosen the sides with a small palette knife before turning out onto a wetted plate.

FRUIT PAVLOVA

SERVES 6
Base
3 large egg whites
a pinch of salt
175g (6 oz) caster sugar
$\frac{1}{2}$ tsp vanilla extract
1 tsp white wine vinegar
1 tsp cornflour
Filling
300ml (10 fl oz) double cream
350g (12 oz) fresh fruit – sliced kiwi fruit, peaches, strawberries or raspberries, or a mixture of two contrasting fruits
Mint or raspberry leaves, to garnish

Use a pencil to draw an 18cm (7 inch) circle on a sheet of baking parchment and place upside down on a cold plain shelf. Alternatively, use a circle of Bake-O-Glide as a larger template. Whisk the egg whites with the salt in a grease-free bowl until stiff. Add the sugar a spoonful at a time whilst still whisking. Finally: mix the vanilla extract with the vinegar and cornflour and whisk in. Spread the mixture out to form a base with an outer crown.

MAIN OVEN 120°C (250°F), GAS MARK L-1
ⓒ LOWER OVEN IN SLOW COOKING MODE
Bake low down in the oven, for 1-2 hours, until crisp on the outside but like marshmallow in the centre. Whip the cream until stiff and pile in the centre of the meringue. Add the fresh fruit and decorate with mint or raspberry leaves.

GOOSEBERRY FOOL

SERVES 6
675g (1$\frac{1}{2}$ lb) green gooseberries, topped and tailed
1 handful fresh young elderflowers, stems removed and florets tied in muslin or 2 tbsp elderflower syrup
175g (6 oz) caster sugar
300ml (10 fl oz) whipped double cream or fromage frais or Greek yoghurt
300ml (10 fl oz) thick custard, made using 25g (1 oz) each custard powder and sugar

Rinse the gooseberries in cold water and place in a pan with the elderflowers or syrup. Cover with a lid and place on the simmering end of the hotplate. Once the juices start to run, adjust the pan so that it is only just on the hotplate, or transfer to a cool oven for 30-45 minutes, until the fruit is cooked. Once cool, remove the elderflowers and mash the fruit. For the smoothest finish, pass through a nylon sieve at this point. Stir in the sugar. Whip the double cream and fold into the fruit purée, or stir in the fromage frais or yoghurt. Finally fold in the custard and place in elegant tall glasses, decorating with a little whipped cream if liked. Chill before serving with almond or hazelnut biscuits.

VARIATIONS
The same recipe can be used with cooked rhubarb, apricot or peaches. Also, uncooked and sieved soft fruit purées, such as raspberry, may be used.

HAZELNUT MERINGUE CAKE

SERVES 6-8
Base
3 large egg whites
A pinch of salt
175g (6 oz) caster sugar
55g (2 oz) hazelnuts, toasted and chopped
Filling and decoration
300ml (10 fl oz) double cream
1 tbsp Camp coffee essence
450g (1 lb) fresh passion fruits

Right
Fruit Pavlova

55g (2 oz) dark chocolate chips
A little drinking chocolate powder

Line two baking sheets with baking parchment and use a pencil to draw a 20cm (8 inch) circle on the undersides of both sheets. Whisk the egg whites with the salt in a grease-free bowl until stiff. Add the sugar, a spoonful at a time whilst still whisking. Finally, fold in the chopped nuts and divide the mixture between the two baking sheets. Use a palette knife to form a pattern on the top of the neater disk.

MAIN OVEN 120°C (250°F), GAS MARK L-1
Ⓒ LOWER OVEN IN SLOW COOKING MODE
Bake one sheet on a grid shelf on the third set of runners down. Bake the neater disk on a grid shelf on the lowest set of runners. Leave to dry out completely and crisp to the centre, this will take 1½-2 hours.

To assemble and decorate, place the unopened packet of chocolate chips on a cool part of the top plate to melt the chocolate. Whip the cream until it is stiff and stir in the coffee essence. Assemble the cake with the coffee cream on the non-patterned meringue. Halve the passion fruits and scoop out their pulp and seeds onto the cream. Carefully top with the patterned meringue, and then lightly dust around the outer edge with the chocolate powder. Finally, cut open the bag of chocolate making a small cut and drizzle the contents in a zigzag pattern across the cake. Assemble and serve on the same day so that the meringue stays as crisp as possible.

OLD ENGLISH TRIFLE

SERVES 6
600ml (1 pint) full-cream milk
1 tsp vanilla extract
2 large eggs
2 large egg yolks
25g (1 oz) caster sugar
8 trifle sponges, or left-over sponge cake
115g (4 oz) jam, raspberry or strawberry
125ml (5 fl oz) medium sherry
1 tbsp Cognac
1 packet raspberry jelly (optional)
115g (4 oz) amaretti biscuits or ratafias
300ml (10 fl oz) double cream
To decorate
55g (2 oz) glacé cherries, halved
40g (1½ oz) toasted flaked almonds

Heat the milk with the vanilla extract until it just reaches boiling point. Beat together the eggs, yolks and sugar. Pour the hot milk over the egg mixture and return to the pan. Cook with the pan just on the simmering end of the hotplate, stirring all the time for about 10 minutes, until the mixture thickens slightly. Take off the heat and leave to cool.

Slice the sponges in half and sandwich together with the jam and place in the base of a 2 litre (3½ pint) glass serving bowl. Spoon over the sherry and Cognac, or use this with water to make up a packet jelly and allow this to set in the sponge base. Next add a layer of the amaretti biscuits or ratafias and pour over the cold custard. Whip the cream until stiff and pile half onto the top of the custard. Pipe the remainder on top and decorate with the cherries and flaked almonds.

STEAMED SPONGE PUDDING FACTORY

SERVES 4-6
Sponge
115g (4 oz) butter or soft margarine
115g (4 oz) caster sugar
175g (6 oz) self raising flour
2 large eggs, beaten
½ tsp vanilla extract
A little milk

Place all of the sponge ingredients apart from the milk in a bowl and beat well with a wooden spoon for 2 minutes. If using a machine, mix for 30 seconds, scraping down once. Finally add a little milk, if necessary, to produce a dropping consistency. Butter a 1.1 litre (2 pint) pudding basin, and place the topping in the base (for suggestions *see* opposite). Pour over the sponge mixture and cover with a pleated disk of both baking parchment and foil and fix securely. Place on a trivet or small enamel plate in a saucepan and pour boiling water to come halfway up the side of the basin. Cover and bring to the boil. Adjust the position on the hotplate to maintain a medium boil for 30 minutes.

MAIN OVEN 120°C (250°F), GAS MARK L-1
Ⓒ LOWER OVEN IN SLOW COOKING MODE
Transfer the pan, pudding and water to the floor of the oven and continue to steam for 1½-2½ hours. No topping up will be required. Alternatively, continue steaming on the hotplate, topping up with boiling water as necessary.

VARIATIONS

CHOCOLATE SPONGE
Substitute 25g (1 oz) of sieved cocoa for this amount of flour, add 1/2 tsp vanilla extract, and serve with chocolate custard or hot Chocolate Sauce (*see* p96)

COFFEE SPONGE
Add 2 tsp Camp coffee essence to the mixture.

GINGER SPONGE
Add 2 tsp ground ginger to the mixture and put a little chopped crystallised ginger with 4 tbsp of golden syrup into the bottom of the basin. Serve with Ginger Sauce, (*see* p96).

JAM SPONGE
Put 4 tbsp jam into the bottom of the basin. Serve with Jam Sauce (*see* p96).

LEMON SPONGE
Put 4 tbsp Lemon Curd (*see* p138) into the bottom of the basin.

SULTANA SPONGE
Add 115g (4 oz) sultanas to the mixture.

SYRUP SPONGE
Put 4 tbsp golden syrup into the bottom of the basin.

TOFFEE SPONGE
Put 4 tbsp Sticky Toffee Sauce (*see* p96) into the bottom of the basin.

LEMON TART

SERVES 8
Pastry
225g (8 oz) plain flour
2 tbsp icing sugar
115g (4 oz) butter
3-4 tbsp cold water
Filling
8 eggs
350g (12 oz) caster sugar
300ml (10 fl oz) double cream
Grated zest of 2 lemons
Juice of 4 lemons
Icing sugar, for dusting

Sift the flour into a mixing bowl. Stir in the icing sugar and cut the butter into dice and rub into the flour or process lightly in a food processor. Add just enough water so that the mixture just starts to cohere. Roll out on a floured board and use to line a 23cm (9 inch) loose-based fluted flan tin. Prick the base with a fork and freeze for an hour.

Place the eggs and sugar in a mixing bowl and beat together until smooth, then add the cream and stir in the lemon zest and juice. Pour into the frozen pastry case.

MAIN OVEN 200°C (400°F), GAS MARK 6
Bake on the floor of the oven for about 30 minutes, with a cold plain shelf on the second set of runners above. Turn halfway through cooking, and place a greased piece of foil loosely over the tart at this point. Bake until the pastry edge is golden and the filling is just set. Remove from the oven and leave to cool completely before removing from the tin. Dust the edge of the tart with a little icing sugar before serving.

LEMON MERINGUE PIE

SERVES 6
Pastry
175g (6 oz) plain flour
85g (3 oz) butter
15g (1/2 oz) icing sugar
1 large egg yolk, beaten
1 tbsp cold water
Filling
2 large unwaxed lemons
40g (1 1/2 oz) cornflour
25g (1 oz) butter
75g (3 oz) caster sugar
2 large egg yolks
Meringue
3 large egg whites
A pinch of salt
50-115g (2-4 oz) caster sugar

Sift the flour into a mixing bowl, then cut the butter into small dice and rub into the flour. Stir in the icing sugar and add the beaten egg yolk and just enough water to mix to firm dough. Turn out and pat into a flattened disk, wrap in clingfilm and chill for 30 minutes. Roll out and line a 23cm (9 inch) deep pie dish or flan case. Prick the base with a fork and freeze for 30 minutes.

MAIN OVEN 200°C (400°F), GAS MARK 6
Bake from frozen on the floor of the oven for 10-15 minutes until a pale golden colour, turning once. Lining with parchment and baking beans will not be necessary.

To make the filling, remove the zest from the lemons and then place the lemons in the Main Oven for 2-3 minutes to warm before juicing. Place the zest, juice and cornflour in a glass measuring jug and make up to 300ml (10 fl oz) with cold water, and stir until blended. Bring to the boil in a pan with the butter and sugar on the boiling end of the hotplate, stirring continuously. Continue to cook on the simmering end of the hotplate, until it has become thick. Remove from the heat and whisk in the egg yolks. Continue to cook on the simmering end of the hotplate, stirring, for a further minute. Allow to cool a little then spread in the pastry case.

Whisk the egg whites with the salt until stiff in a grease-free bowl, then add the sugar a teaspoonful at a time whilst still whisking. If serving hot, 50g (2 oz) of sugar is required. If serving cold, a larger quantity of sugar gives a better result. Pipe or pile on top to completely cover the lemon filling, then place the pie in the centre of the Main Oven for 3-5 minutes until the top of the pie is a very light golden colour, with the peaks slightly darkened. To serve hot, transfer to the Lower Oven for 15-20 minutes, the top should be slightly crisp giving way to a softer meringue centre. To serve cold, allow an hour in the Lower Oven to cook the meringue further before cooling.

PANCAKES

SERVES 4
Batter
115g (4 oz) plain flour
1 large egg
300ml (10 fl oz) milk
55g (2 oz) melted butter
To serve
Fresh lemons
Caster sugar
Maple or *golden syrup*

Mix the egg into the flour with a wooden spoon then gradually add the milk to form a smooth batter. Alternatively, use a food processor and whiz all the ingredients for a few seconds, scrape down and process again. Before making the pancakes, place the butter in a ramekin on the top plate to melt.

Heat a crêpe pan on the boiling end of the hotplate for a good minute. Pour in a little butter, swirl it around and pour back the excess. Wipe the pan with a piece of kitchen paper and spoon in a ladleful of the batter, immediately tip the pan to allow the batter to run around and form a pancake. Once it has set, loosen at the edges and turn with a palette knife. If making a batch, lightly oil the simmering end of the hotplate and the second sides may be cooked here while you start to make the next pancake in the pan on the boiling end of the hotplate.

PEARS POACHED IN WINE

SERVES 6
1 x 750ml bottle red wine
175g (6 oz) caster sugar
1 cinnamon stick
2.5cm (1 inch) piece of root ginger, peeled
1 strip orange peel, pith removed
6 large pears, peeled, not quite ripe
3 tbsp crème de cassis

Pour the wine into a pan and add the sugar, spices and orange peel. Heat slowly on the simmering end of the hotplate and simmer gently for 20 minutes. Peel, halve and core the pears, leaving the stalks intact. Fit the pears snugly in the pan and bring to a simmer.

MAIN OVEN 150°C (300°F), GAS MARK 2
🄖 LOWER OVEN IN SLOW COOKING MODE

Cover and transfer to the floor of the oven to simmer slowly for 15-25 minutes, until tender. Alternatively, continue to simmer with the pan just on the simmering end of the hotplate.

Remove the pears to a serving dish, add the crème de cassis and bring to a boil until syrupy and reduced by about a third. Pour over the pears and refrigerate before serving cold.

VARIATION
In place of the crème de cassis use white wine with the same aromatics, plus a few strands of saffron for colour and flavour.

POACHED FRUIT

SERVES 4-6
Fresh Fruit
450g (1 lb) fresh firm fruit, e.g. apples, apricots,
*   gooseberries, peaches, pears, plums, rhubarb*
55-115g (2-4 oz) sugar
300ml (10 fl oz) water or fruit juice

The amount of sugar needed will depend on the fruit
being stewed. Fruit may be stewed in very little water
at very low temperatures to retain perfect flavour and
texture. If preferred, sweeten with honey instead of
sugar. Apple juice makes a perfect poaching medium
for many fruits, requiring little extra sweetening.

Slowly dissolve the sugar in the water or fruit juice in
a pan on the simmering end of the hotplate. Once the
sugar has dissolved, bring to the boil and slow boil for
a couple of minutes. Add the fruit and return the pan to
the simmering end of the hotplate. Once the liquid has
maintained a simmer for 5 minutes, transfer the pan to
the Lower Oven (all models) for 20-90 minutes, until the
fruit is tender. Time will depend on the type of fruit and
cooker setting.

VARIATIONS
The following flavour pairings particularly compliment
different fruits:

APPLE
Add a little lemon juice and zest to the fruit.
APRICOT
Crack open a few stones and add the apricot kernels.
GOOSEBERRY
Lace with a little elderflower syrup.
PEACH
Add a little brandy after cooking and cooling the fruit.
PEAR
Add a piece of cinnamon stick during cooking.
PLUM
Drizzle with a little stem ginger syrup.
RHUBARB
Cook in a little reduced orange juice.

DRIED FRUIT
Follow the recipe for Poached Fruit Compôte (*see p28*).

PROFITEROLES

SERVES 4
150ml (5 fl oz) water
55g (2 oz) butter
65g (2½ oz) strong or plain flour
2 eggs, beaten
Filling
300ml (½ pint) double cream

Place the water and butter in a saucepan on the
simmering end of the hotplate. Sieve the flour onto a
sheet of baking parchment. Bring the saucepan to the
boil and then pour the flour into the mixture all in one
go. Stir for a minute with a wooden spoon on the
simmering end of the hotplate until the mixture forms
a ball. Take off the heat and gradually beat in the eggs.
Place in a piping bag fitted with a 1cm (½ inch) plain
nozzle and pipe 24 small buns onto baking parchment
or Bake-O-Glide on two baking sheets.

MAIN OVEN 220°C (425°F), GAS MARK 7
Bake in the centre of the oven for 15-20 minutes, until
crisp. Cut a slit in each profiterole to allow steam to
escape as they cool. Fill with cream and cover with hot
Chocolate Sauce (*see p96*).

QUEEN OF PUDDINGS

SERVES 4-6
5 tbsp raspberry jam
600ml (1 pint) milk
55g (2 oz) butter
½ tsp vanilla extract
175g (6 oz) fresh white breadcrumbs
25g (1 oz) caster sugar
Zest of 1 lemon, finely grated
4 large eggs
A pinch of salt
115g (4 oz) caster sugar

Place the jam jar with the lid loosened on the top plate
to warm ready for spreading. In a pan bring the milk,
butter and vanilla extract to the boil on the hotplate and
add the breadcrumbs. Stir in the sugar and lemon zest
and remove from the heat. Leave to cool for 10 minutes
then separate the eggs and beat the yolks into the milk
and breadcrumb mixture. Pour into a 1.7 litre (3 pint)
buttered pie dish and leave to stand for 30 minutes.

MAIN OVEN 150°C (300°F), GAS MARK 2
Bake in the middle of the oven for 50-60 minutes, until set. Allow to cool slightly then spread with the jam. Whisk the egg whites with the salt until stiff, then add the sugar in spoonfuls whilst still whisking. Pile on top of the custard and return to the top of the oven for 15-20 minutes until the meringue is set and just coloured.

VARIATION

For an Apricot Queen of Puddings, replace the raspberry jam with a layer of tinned apricot (without the juice) or cooled, stewed fresh apricots before topping with the meringue.

RICE PUDDING

SERVES 4-6
55g (2 oz) short-grain pudding rice
55g (2 oz) caster sugar
25g (1 oz) butter
1.2 litres (2 pints) full-fat milk
Freshly grated nutmeg

The creamier the milk the creamier the pudding. Adding a small can of evaporated milk improves this recipe enormously, or try using Channel Island milk. Generously butter a 1.5 litre ($2^{3}/_{4}$ pint) ovenproof dish. Fill with the rice, sugar and rest of the butter and pour over the milk. Stir a little and grate some nutmeg over the top.

MAIN OVEN 150°C (300°F), GAS MARK 2
ⓒ LOWER OVEN IN SLOW COOKING MODE
Bake for 2-3 hours, or start off with 30 minutes in a hotter oven and transfer to the Lower Oven to finish cooking over several hours, checking to obtain your preferred consistency. May also be slow-cooked, tightly covered with foil, on the floor of the Main Oven at an idling setting.

VARIATIONS

Macaroni, tapioca or sago may all be cooked with this method.

REGENCY APPLE PIE

SERVES 6
Pastry
350g (12 oz) plain flour
2 tbsp icing sugar
85g (3 oz) butter
85g (3 oz) vegetable shortening
4-6 tbsp cold water
Filling
675g ($1^{1}/_{2}$ lb) cooking apples
Finely grated zest of $^{1}/_{2}$ a lemon
115g (4 oz) Demerara sugar
1 tbsp plain flour
A pinch of grated nutmeg
$^{1}/_{4}$ tsp ground cinnamon
15g ($^{1}/_{2}$ oz) butter, melted
55g (2 oz) sultanas (optional)
Caster sugar, to dredge

Sift the flour into a mixing bowl and add the icing sugar. Cut the fats into pieces and lightly rub into the flour. Add just enough water to mix to firm dough. Turn out and pat into two flattened disks, one slightly larger than the other, wrap in clingfilm and chill for 30 minutes. Roll out the larger disk of pastry and line a 23cm (9 inch) deep pie dish. Peel and core the apples, then slice thickly into a large mixing bowl. Add the other filling ingredients and toss well to coat the apple slices. Pile into the pastry case and roll out the remaining pastry. Brush the edge of the pie with water and cover with the lid, sealing the edge and crimping using a table knife and finger and thumb. Make two cuts to let the steam escape, brush with a little water and dredge with caster sugar.

MAIN OVEN 190°C (375°F), GAS MARK 5
Bake in the centre of the oven for 35-40 minutes until the fruit is tender and the top is golden brown. Serve warm.

SLOW-COOKED CHEESECAKE

SERVES 6-8
Base
55g (2 oz) butter, melted
115g (4 oz) digestive biscuits, crushed
1 tsp finely grated lemon zest
25-55g (1-2 oz) caster sugar
Topping
55g (2 oz) butter
85g (3 oz) caster sugar
1 tsp finely grated lemon zest
3 large eggs
3 tbsp lemon juice
450g (1 lb) cream or curd cheese
3 tbsp single cream
a pinch of salt

Lightly grease a 23cm (9 inch) loose-bottomed spring form tin. Mix the butter with the crumbs, lemon zest and sugar. Press into the base of the tin.

Cream the butter, sugar and lemon zest until soft and light. Separate the eggs and gradually beat the yolks into the creamed mixture. Stir in the lemon juice, cheese and cream. Whisk the egg whites with the salt until they are stiff. Stir a tablespoon of the whites into the mixture to slacken it and then gently fold in the rest.

MAIN OVEN 150°C (300°F), GAS MARK 2
On a grid shelf on the lowest set of runners bake for 1-1¼ hours, until the cheesecake is just firm. Transfer to the Lower Oven (all models) for 30 minutes to finish setting. When completely cold, unmould from the tin. Serve with fresh or well-drained tinned fruit, and decorate with whipped cream.

STRAWBERRY SHORTCAKE

SERVES 6-8
140g (5 oz) butter, softened
175g (6 oz) caster sugar
3 medium-sized eggs
225g (8 oz) self raising flour
Filling and decoration
300ml (10 fl oz) double cream
450g (1 lb) strawberries
2-3 tbsp redcurrant jelly
A little caster sugar

Lightly grease and flour two 20cm (8 inch) sandwich tins. Cream the butter and sugar until light and fluffy then gradually beat in the eggs, a dessertspoonful at a time. Sift the flour and fold into the mixture. Mix well to a softish dough and divide in two. Roll out to make two 20cm (8 inch) circles and press these into the tins, marking one into 6 or 8 petticoat tail shapes.

MAIN OVEN 180°C (350°F), GAS MARK 4
Bake on a grid shelf on the lowest set of runners for about 25 minutes until light golden and firm. Cool in the tins for 10 minutes before carefully turning out and cooling on a wire rack.

Lightly whip the cream so that it just holds its shape. Halve the strawberries and toss in a bowl with the redcurrant jelly and a little sugar. Spread two-thirds of the cream on the plain circle and top with most of the strawberries. Pipe or spoon some cream equally in 6 or 8 positions on top of the fruit and arrange the petticoat-tail pieces around the shortcake to give a fanned effect. Dust with a little extra caster sugar and decorate with a halved strawberry on the top of each portion. Note: it's best to assemble the shortcake just before eating to prevent the cake becoming soft.

SUSSEX POND PUDDING

SERVES 8
225g (8 oz) self raising flour
115g (4 oz) shredded suet
150ml (5 fl oz) milk and water, mixed
115g (4 oz) butter
115g (4 oz) light soft brown sugar
1 large lemon, un-waxed and thin-skinned

Sieve the flour into a mixing bowl and add the suet, mixing well. Add enough of the liquid to form a soft but not wet dough. Generously butter a 1.4-1.7 litre (2½-3 pint) pudding basin. Roll the dough into a large circle and cut out a quarter to save to make a lid. Use the remaining dough to line the basin. Wet the edges with a little cold water to seal the cut edges. Cut the butter into small dice and place half in the basin with half the sugar. Prick the whole lemon deeply all over using a thick skewer. Place on top of the butter and sugar and cover with the remainder of the butter and sugar. Roll out the reserved pastry to make a lid. Attach to the pastry lining using a little cold water and crimp the join firmly. Cover with a pleated disk of both baking parchment and foil and fix securely. Place on a trivet or small enamel plate in a saucepan and pour boiling water to come halfway up the side of the basin. Cover and bring to the boil. Adjust the position on the hotplate to maintain a medium boil for 30 minutes.

MAIN OVEN 120°C (250°F), GAS MARK L-1
Ⓒ LOWER OVEN IN SLOW COOKING MODE
Transfer the pan, water and pudding to the floor of the oven to continue to steam for a further 3 hours where no topping up will be required. Alternatively, continue steaming on the hotplate, topping up with boiling water as necessary. To serve, turn onto a shallow dish. As it is sliced, the rich lemon sauce will pour out into the dish. Each portion should include a share of the suet crust, tender lemon and buttery sauce.

VARIATION
KENTISH WELL PUDDING
Follow the recipe above, but replace the lemon with 175g (6 oz) currants.

STICKY TOFFEE PUDDING

SERVES 8
225g (8 oz) stoned chopped dates
300ml (10 fl oz) boiling water
115g (4 oz) soft butter
175g (6 oz) soft brown sugar
225g (8 oz) self raising flour
4 large eggs, beaten
1 tsp bicarbonate of soda
1 tbsp Camp coffee essence
To decorate
3 tbsp chopped pecan nuts

Pour the boiling water over the dates and leave to soak with the pan on the warm top plate for five minutes before removing and leaving to cool a little. Cream the fat and the sugar together thoroughly. Sieve the flour and stir a tablespoon into the butter and sugar mixture before gradually adding the beaten egg a tablespoon at a time. Fold in the remainder of the flour. Add the bicarbonate of soda and coffee essence to the slightly cooled dates and water and stir into the mixture to form a soft batter.

MAIN OVEN 180°C (350°F), GAS MARK 4
Pour into a well-buttered 25cm (10 inch) oval baking dish and cook on a grid shelf on the lowest set of runners for 1¼-1½ hours. Top with some Sticky Toffee Sauce (*see* p96) and sprinkle with the nuts. Return to a hot oven to heat through and allow the sauce to bubble before serving with extra sticky toffee sauce.

SUMMER PUDDING

As well as trying the usual mixture of soft fruits, it is worth experimenting using fewer fruits. The late Elizabeth David's recipe calls for a mixture of just raspberries and redcurrants though other combinations make equally delightful variations.

SERVES 4-6
675g (1½ lbs) fresh or frozen mixed soft fruits, such as redcurrants, blackcurrants, raspberries, strawberries, blackberries, blueberries, etc.
4 tbsp blackcurrant cordial or crème de framboises
25-55g (1-2 oz) caster sugar to taste
8-10 slices of medium-sliced day-old white bread, 1cm (½ inch) thick, (alternatively, slices of leftover cake, including Panettone, can be used)
To decorate
Mint or raspberry leaves

Place the fruits in a stainless steel or enamelled pan with the cordial or liqueur and place on the simmering end of the hotplate, stirring occasionally. Heat up to allow the juices to run, cook just long enough for the fruit to become just tender, this will vary depending on the fruits chosen. Then slowly add sugar to taste, but avoid over-sweetening. Rinse out a 1.1 litre (2 pint) basin or charlotte mould with cold water and line with two long pieces of clingfilm, arranged crossways. Remove the crusts from the bread and trim into tapered rectangular shapes.

Place a disk of bread in the base of the lined basin and then arrange the tapered pieces overlapping to line the sides. Reserve two pieces to act as a lid. Pour the warmed fruit into the lined basin, adding any remaining bread offcuts in the middle to make a centre layer.

Right
Sticky Toffee Pudding

Reserve 3-5 tbsp of the juice. Place the bread lid pieces on top and close the ends of the clingfilm across the top of the pudding to seal it. Place a plate on top of the clingfilm and stand in the refrigerator in a tray to catch any drips. Place some heavy weights, such as large tins, on the plate to press the pudding and leave to go quite cold before serving (at least 6 hours – overnight is ideal). When the pudding is released from its mould, brush the reserved fruit juice over any bare patches of bread before decorating with mint or raspberry leaves.

TARTE TATIN

SERVES 6
115g (4 oz) plain flour
85g (3 oz) butter
1 tbsp icing sugar
2-3 tbsp cold water
Filling
55g (2 oz) butter
55g (2 oz) soft brown sugar
900g (2 lbs) dessert apples
Juice of 1 lemon

Sift the flour into a mixing bowl and cut the fat into small dice and rub into the flour. Add just enough water to mix to firm dough. Turn out and pat into a flattened disk, wrap in clingfilm and chill for 30 minutes. Roll out into a 20cm (8 inch) circle. Place the butter and sugar into a 20cm (8 inch) pan and place on the simmering end of the hotplate. Stir occasionally to allow the butter to melt and the sugar to dissolve. Peel, core and slice the apples fairly thickly. Arrange the slices in the pan slightly overlapping in several circles and sprinkle over the lemon juice. Place the disk of pastry on top of the apples and transfer to the boiling end of the hotplate. Leave for 2 minutes before transferring to the oven.

MAIN OVEN 190°C (375°F), GAS MARK 5
Bake on the floor of the oven for 20-25 minutes until a light golden brown. Carefully inspect the edges to see how golden the caramel has become. If necessary, return the pan to the boiling end of the hotplate for a couple of minutes to finish cooking the caramel to a golden colour. Allow to cool for a few minutes before turning out upside down onto a warm plate.

TREACLE TART

SERVES 6
Pastry
225g (8 oz) plain flour
A pinch of salt
115g (4oz) butter or margarine
2 tbsp cold water
Filling
350g (12 oz) golden syrup
115g (4 oz) white breadcrumbs
$\frac{1}{2}$ tsp ground ginger
Finely grated zest and juice of 1 lemon

Place the syrup in a bowl on the warm top plate while you make the pastry. Sift the flour into a mixing bowl, then add the salt and cut the fat into small dice and rub into the flour. Add just enough water to mix to firm dough. Turn out and pat into a flattened disk, wrap in clingfilm and chill for 30 minutes. Roll out thinly and line a 20cm (8 inch) deep pie plate or flan dish, saving any trimming for decoration if liked. Prick the pastry case well with a fork.

Stir the breadcrumbs and ginger into the warmed syrup and add the lemon zest and juice. Spread over the pastry and roll out any extra pastry and cut into 1cm ($\frac{1}{2}$ inch) strips and twist and place in the traditional lattice pattern.

MAIN OVEN 190°C (375°F), GAS MARK 5
Bake on the floor of the oven for 20 minutes, then transfer to a grid shelf on the lowest set of runners for a further 10-15 minutes, until the pastry is a light golden and the filling just set.

VARIATION
For a thinner tart, line a pie plate with the pastry and use half the quantity of filling.

HOME BAKING

Home baking and the Rayburn are truly great partners, complementing each other perfectly. Whether cooking a rich fruit cake slowly or baking cranberry scones quickly, the radiant heat of the cast-iron oven ensures the finished result is moist and delicious.

The warmth of the Rayburn during a baking session has many uses; warming flour for bread making, melting chocolate for decorating biscuits and cakes or softening butter to make creaming easier. When you need to grease a cake tin, just put a little butter in the base of the tin and put it on the top plate to melt, then brush over the tin – this saves melting the butter separately. A cork mat or a piece of folded kitchen paper under the tin will protect the enamel, remove the mat or paper when you remove the tin.

The Rayburn meat tin is ideal for baking traybakes, (large sheet cakes), they're a wonderful way to feed a lot of people for minimum effort. Just one of these cakes will cut into approximately 24-36 pieces, and are ideal for cake stall fund raising activities.

BANANA AND CHOCOLATE CAKE

This recipe, from Tricia Dunbar, is a winner at Rayburn Demonstrations. It's an easy to make moist cake cooked in the meat tin. It also keeps very well.

CUTS INTO 24 OR 36 SQUARES
450g (1 lb) self raising flour
1 level tsp baking powder
325g (11 oz) soft brown sugar
175g (6 oz) butter, softened
3 large eggs
1 tsp vanilla extract
6 ripe bananas, these can be black!
6-8 tbsp milk
200g bar of good plain chocolate

Measure the flour, baking powder, sugar, butter, eggs, vanilla extract and bananas into a bowl and use a potato masher to squash the mixture together, mixing it well.

Add enough milk to make a dropping consistency. Cut each of the chocolate squares into 4-6 pieces – the easiest way to do this is to leave the chocolate bar at room temperature for 10 minutes then place the unwrapped bar onto a chopping board and with a large knife cut the bar along the grooves both ways. Then chop each square into quarters again cutting them all across in long lines, rather than cutting each square. Stir the chocolate into the cake mixture.

Line the Rayburn meat tin with Bake-O-Glide and spoon in the mixture.

MAIN OVEN 190°C (375°F), GAS MARK 5
Slide the tin onto the centre set of runners and cook for about 45 minutes.

Cool in the tin for 20 minutes then turn out onto a cake rack to cool completely.

BANANA AND WALNUT LOAF CAKE

MAKES 1 X 1 LB LOAF
115g (4 oz) butter
115g (4 oz) caster sugar
2 ripe bananas, mashed
115g (4 oz) self raising flour
85g (3 oz) wholemeal flour
$1/2$ tsp baking powder
1 egg, beaten
55g (2 oz) walnuts, chopped

Grease a 450g (1 lb) loaf tin and line with a strip of baking parchment.

Cream the butter and sugar together until soft and fluffy. Mix in the mashed bananas. Fold in the self raising flour, wholemeal flour, baking powder and egg, then fold in the walnuts. Put the mixture into the loaf tin.

MAIN OVEN 180°C (350°F), GAS MARK 4
Cook just below the centre of the oven for about 50 minutes.

Cool for 15 minutes then remove from the tin and cool on a wire rack. Cut into slices to serve.

CHOCOLATE ORANGE CAKE

CUTS INTO 6-8
115g (4 oz) self raising flour
25g (1 oz) cocoa
1 tsp baking powder
115g (4 oz) soft margarine
85g (3 oz) caster sugar
25g (1 oz) golden syrup
Grated zest of 1 orange, plus 2 tbsp juice
2 eggs, beaten
55g (2 oz) plain chocolate chips
Decoration
25g (1 oz) chopped walnuts

Place all the cake ingredients into a basin and beat thoroughly. Turn into a greased 18cm (7 inch) round tin. Sprinkle over the chopped walnuts.

MAIN OVEN AT 180°C (350°F), GAS MARK 4
Bake in the centre of the oven for about 40-45 minutes until risen and cooked through.

Rest in the tin for 10 minutes then turn out and cool on a wire rack.

VARIATION

Substitute the chopped walnut decoration for a buttercream topping, smooth onto the cake after it has cooled. Use 15g ($^1/_2$ oz) cocoa mixed with 2 tbsp hot water. Into this, beat 40g (1$^1/_2$ oz) softened butter and 85g (3 oz) icing sugar. Decorate with curls of chocolate.

COTTAGE CHEESE GRIDDLE CAKES

These light griddle cakes are lovely served either sweet with honey, or as a savoury with cream cheese and a tomato relish.

MAKES 8
25g (1 oz) butter
115g (4 oz) cottage cheese
2 eggs, beaten
55g (2 oz) wholemeal self raising flour
3 tbsp milk

Melt the butter in a basin on the Rayburn top plate, use a little cork mat to protect the enamel.

Beat the cottage cheese, eggs, flour and milk to form a thick batter.

HOTPLATE
Lightly oil a piece of kitchen towel and use to oil the simmering to moderate side of the hotplate. Drop tablespoons of the mixture onto the surface. Cook until just set, then turn over and cook the other side.

Transfer to a wire rack (the Rayburn grill rack is ideal) and cover with a clean tea towel, to keep warm and soft. Serve warm.

DROP SCONES

These scones are cooked direct on the hotplate on a simmering to moderate heat. They are also known as Scotch Pancakes, Griddle Scones, Crempog or just plain Pancakes!

MAKES 20
115g (4 oz) self raising flour
25g (1 oz) caster sugar
1 egg
150ml ($^1/_4$ pint) milk
To serve
Butter

Place the flour and sugar into a basin, mix together. Make a well in the centre and add the egg and half the milk. Whisk together, adding the remainder of the milk to make a smooth batter.

Lightly oil the simmering side of the hotplate (with a little oil on a piece of kitchen paper) then drop tablespoonfuls of the mixture onto the surface. Cook one side then flip over and cook the other. Keep warm in a clean tea towel and serve buttered.

FARMHOUSE FRUIT CAKE

CUTS INTO 6-8
115g (4 oz) wholemeal flour
115g (4 oz) plain white flour
2 tsp baking powder
1 tsp nutmeg, grated
85g (3 oz) butter
85g (3 oz) soft brown sugar
175g (6 oz) sultanas
55g (2 oz) mixed peel
55g (2 oz) glacé cherries, quartered
$^1/_2$ lemon
2 eggs, beaten
150ml ($^1/_4$ pint) milk

Mix together the flours, baking powder and nutmeg. Rub in the butter until the mixture resembles breadcrumbs, or use a food processor to do this.

Stir in the sugar, sultanas, peel, cherries and the zest and juice of the half lemon. Make a well in the mixture and add the eggs and milk, mix together. Spoon the cake mixture into a greased and lined 18cm (7 inch) round cake tin.

MAIN OVEN 180°C (350°F), GAS MARK 4
Bake for about 1$^1/_4$ hours just below the centre of the oven, until the cake is browned and firm to the touch.

Allow to cool for 15 minutes then turn out onto a cake rack to cool completely.

COFFEE AND WALNUT TRAYBAKE

CUTS INTO 16-24 OR 36 SQUARES
350g (12 oz) soft margarine
350g (12 oz) caster sugar
4 eggs
450g (1 lb) self raising flour
1$^1/_2$ tsp baking powder
4 tsp coffee granules in 2 tbsp hot water
175g (6 oz) walnuts, chopped
Icing
115g (4 oz) butter, melted
3 tsp coffee granules
2 tbsp hot water
350g (12 oz) icing sugar
Decoration
Walnut halves

Place all ingredients for the cake into a basin and beat well together. Pour into the Rayburn meat tin, lined with Bake-O-Glide.

MAIN OVEN 180°C (350°F), GAS MARK 4
Slide the tin onto the middle set of runners and bake for about 40 minutes, or until the cake is risen and golden.

Remove the tin from the oven and cool on a wire rack. When the cake is cool cover with the icing.

To make the icing, melt the butter in a bowl on the top plate of the Rayburn (use a little cork mat to protect the enamel). Dissolve the coffee in the hot water and add this with the icing sugar to the butter, beat together well and place on the cake – the icing thickens on cooling. Mark a pattern with a palette knife and decorate with walnut halves. Cut into squares when cool.

GINGER CAKE

CUTS INTO 36 SQUARES
175g (6 oz) butter
225ml (8 fl oz) golden syrup
225ml (8 fl oz) black treacle
115g (4 oz) brown sugar
4 tsp ground ginger
450g (1 lb) plain flour
1 level tsp bicarbonate of soda
A pinch of salt
3 eggs, beaten
225ml (8 fl oz) milk
Topping
200g (7 oz) icing sugar
3 tbsp lemon juice

Line the Rayburn meat tin with Bake-O-Glide.

Melt the butter, syrup, treacle and sugar together in a saucepan on the hotplate. Sieve the ginger, flour, bicarbonate of soda and salt in a large bowl. Make a well in the centre and add the eggs, milk and melted ingredients. Whisk the ingredients with a wire whisk, slowly, to avoid any lumps of flour. Place in the tin.

MAIN OVEN 180°C (350°F), GAS MARK 4
Slide the tin on the oven grid shelf set on the third set of runners and cook for about 30-35 minutes until the cake has risen and is cooked through.

Remove the cake from the oven and leave for about 20 minutes before placing on a wire rack to cool completely. Mix the icing sugar with enough lemon juice to make it the consistency of thin cream then drizzle this over the cooled cake. This gives a thin coating of icing.

VARIATIONS
• Add 55g (2 oz) of finely chopped glacé ginger to the uncooked mixture.
• Add 55g (2 oz) golden sultanas to the uncooked mixture.

Right
Coffee and Walnut Traybake

MERINGUES

If the meringues become coloured to your liking but are still soft at the base, either move them to the floor of the oven for 30 minutes, or place them on top of the Rayburn insulated lid for 3-4 hours or overnight (protect the lid with a chef's pad).

MAKES 16-20 MINI MERINGUES
2 egg whites
115g (4 oz) caster sugar
Filling
125ml (5 fl oz) carton double cream, whipped or full-fat crème fraîche
Decoration
Icing sugar, sifted

Whisk the egg whites until stiff, the mixture should not come out of the bowl if it is turned upside down. Gradually whisk in the caster sugar a teaspoon at a time. Pipe or spoon individual meringues onto Bake-O-Glide or baking parchment placed on the plain shelf.

MAIN OVEN 120°C (250°F), GAS MARK L-1
Slide the shelf onto the lowest set of runners. Dry out in the low oven for about 2 hours. Cool.

Sandwich the whipped double cream or crème fraîche between the meringue halves, and dredge with sifted icing sugar.

VARIATIONS
- Substitute brown sugar for the caster sugar for coffee-coloured meringues with a caramelised flavour.
- Pipe the meringue mixture into nest shapes, cook and fill with crème fraîche and raspberries for a dessert.
- Colour the meringue mixture with 1-2 drops of pink colouring.

LIME AND COCONUT CAKES

MAKES 12 OR 24 MINIS
115g (4 oz) butter, softened
115g (4 oz) caster sugar
115g (4 oz) self raising flour
2 eggs
25g (1 oz) desiccated coconut
1 lime, zest and juice
Topping

2 tbsp caster sugar
1 lime, zest and juice

Place all the cake ingredients into a basin and beat well together. Divide between cake cases, placed in a bun tray or mini-muffin tins.

MAIN OVEN 180°C (350°F), GAS MARK 4
Cook for about 15 minutes in the centre of the oven. Turn the tin if necessary.

For the topping, mix together the sugar and lime juice, spoon over the top of the cakes. Sprinkle with the lime zest.

VELVET PASTRY MINCE PIES

MAKES 24
450g (1 lb) plain flour
200g (7 oz) butter
85g (3 oz) vegetable shortening
Grated zest of 1 large orange
Chilled orange juice
350-450g (12 oz-1 lb) mincemeat
1 Bramley apple, peeled and grated
55g (2 oz) glacé cherries, finely chopped
2-4 tbsp brandy
Milk

Sift the flour and rub in the fats until the mixture resembles breadcrumbs. Stir in the grated zest and bind with the juice. If using a food processor, take care not to over-process. Chill for 30 minutes before using. Roll and cut out 24 x 5.5cm (2$\frac{1}{4}$ inch) lids first. Then cut out 24 x 7.5cm (3 inch) bases, re-rolling as necessary. Grease the tins lightly and line with the bases. Stir the apple, cherries and brandy into the mincemeat, and add just enough to each pie before topping with a lid, using milk to stick it securely on. Brush with milk and make a small slit in each pie.

MAIN OVEN 200°C (400°F), GAS MARK 6
Bake on the grid shelf in the middle of the oven for 20-30 minutes until golden. Because the pastry is wonderfully crumbly. It is sensible to freeze the pies uncooked. They are then easy to bake from frozen as required.

VARIATIONS

STREUSEL TOPPING
Rub 55g (2 oz) self raising flour, 55g (2 oz) butter, 25g

(1 oz) semolina, 25g (1 oz) caster sugar together until the mixture resembles fine breadcrumbs. Carefully scatter as a topping over each pie and press down lightly before baking.

MACAROON TOPPING
Whisk 2 egg whites until stiff. Add 85g (3 oz) of caster sugar by the spoonful and then fold in 115g (4 oz) ground almonds. Pipe or spoon onto the mincemeat then cook on the grid shelf on the lowest set of runners in a hot Main Oven for 12-15 minutes until golden.

LEMON ICING TOPPING
Warm a lemon in the Main Oven for 2 minutes. Squeeze and strain the juice. Add enough sieved icing sugar to make a thin pouring consistency whilst quite warm. Chill the cooked open pies and then drizzle over the warm icing and place in the refrigerator to allow the icing to set.

MARZIPAN APPLIQUE TOPPING
Roll out some thin marzipan and use small Christmas tree and star cutters to make abstract shapes to top the pies – or use smaller cutters to cut shaped windows in the lids.

MERINGUE TOPPING
Whisk an egg white until stiff, then add 55g (2 oz) caster sugar, a teaspoonful at a time until thick and glossy. Bake the pies until the pastry is golden. Pipe or spoon on the meringue and allow to set in the Lower Oven for 30 minutes.

RASPBERRY AND ALMOND ROLL

A light almond sponge filled with luscious raspberry conserve. Easy to roll due to the radiant cooking heat associated with a cast-iron oven, that doesn't dry out the sponge.

CUTS INTO 8
3 large eggs
85g (3 oz) caster sugar
25g (1 oz) plain flour
55g (2 oz) ground almonds
A little caster sugar
Filling
6 tbsp raspberry conserve
Decoration
Sifted icing sugar

Line and grease a Swiss roll tin 23cm x 33cm (9 inch x 13 inch) with baking parchment, or use Bake-O-Glide.

Whisk the eggs and sugar together until very thick and creamy. Fold in the flour and the ground almonds. Pour into the prepared Swiss roll tin. Lightly level the surface.

MAIN OVEN 220°C (425°F), GAS MARK 7
Cook in the centre of the oven for 6-8 minutes until set and browned, turn the tin once if necessary.

Warm the raspberry conserve by placing in the Lower Oven for about 10 minutes.

Remove the tin from the oven and turn the sponge onto a piece of greaseproof paper sprinkled with a little caster sugar. Make a nick along the long edge of the sponge, about 1cm (1/2 inch) from the edge. Spread the raspberry conserve over the sponge and roll up from the long side. Cool on a wire rack.

Serve on the same day sprinkled with icing sugar and cut into slices.

TRIPLE CHOCOLATE BROWNIES

MAKES 24 OR 36 SQUARES
175g (6 oz) plain chocolate, melted
350g (12 oz) soft brown sugar
140g (5 oz) softened butter
200g (7 oz) cream cheese
175g (6 oz) self raising flour
1 1/2 tbsp cocoa
1 tsp vanilla extract
4 large eggs, beaten
175g (6 oz) walnuts, chopped
200g (7 oz) white chocolate chips

Melt the chocolate in a large bowl on the top plate, placing a cork mat under to protect the enamel. Line the Rayburn meat tin with Bake-O-Glide. Place all the remaining ingredients into the bowl of melted chocolate and mix well together. Pour into the tin.

MAIN OVEN 180°C (350°F), GAS MARK 4
Slide the tin onto the third set of runners down and bake for 30-40 minutes until risen and springy to the touch. Turn the tin halfway during cooking.

Cool on a wire rack and cut into squares.

LEMON VICTORIA SANDWICH

MAKES 6-8 SLICES
175g (6 oz) butter
175g (6 oz) caster sugar
Grated zest of 1 lemon and 1 tbsp of juice
3 eggs, beaten
175g (6 oz) self raising flour
Filling
Lemon curd
Icing sugar to decorate

Cream the butter and sugar together with the grated lemon zest, until light and fluffy. Gradually beat in the eggs. Fold in the flour and a tablespoon of lemon juice. Divide the mixture between two 18cm (7 inch) base lined cake tins.

MAIN OVEN 180°C (350°F), GAS MARK 4
Place one tin on the third set of runners down, and one on the fifth, bake for about 20 minutes, change the cake tins over when the mixture has set.

Cool and sandwich together with lemon curd and dredge with icing sugar.

VARIATIONS
- For a traditional Victoria Sandwich, omit the lemon and use raspberry conserve as a filling, and use caster sugar, instead of icing sugar, to sprinkle on the top.
- For an Orange Victoria Sandwich, substitute an orange for the lemon and sandwich together with orange curd.
- Substitute wholemeal self raising flour for white self raising flour.
- For a chocolate cake, replace 25g (1 oz) of the flour with sieved cocoa (not drinking chocolate).
- Sandwich together with whipped cream, or full-fat crème fraîche and strawberries for a simple gâteau.

MUFFIN FACTORY

Ideas aplenty with a basic recipe which can be adapted, depending upon your tastes and available ingredients!

AMERICAN PLAIN MUFFINS

MAKES 12 LARGE MUFFINS (7CM DIAMETER)
Basic mixture
450g (1 lb) plain flour
6 tsp baking powder
115g (4 oz) caster sugar
1 tsp salt
2 eggs, beaten
2 tsp vanilla extract
300ml ($^1/_2$ pint) milk
55g (2 oz) melted butter

Sift the flour, baking powder, sugar and salt into a basin and mixture together. Add the eggs, vanilla, milk and melted butter and mix together with a fork, the mixture will be lumpy. Place large muffin cases into the muffin tin. Divide the mixture between the muffin cases.

MAIN OVEN 190-200°C (375-400°F), GAS MARK 5-6
Place the muffin tins onto the grid shelf set on the centre runners and bake for 18-20 minutes until golden brown, well risen and cooked through.

As the muffins are fragile whilst hot, leave in the muffin tin for 15 minutes before taking them out. Muffins are best eaten warm.

VARIATIONS

BLACKCURRANT MUFFINS
Take the basic muffin recipe and place half the mixture in the muffin cases then add a dollop (a good teaspoon) of blackcurrant jam. Top with the remaining muffin mixture.

CHOCOLATE MUFFINS
Replace 55g (2 oz) of the plain flour with the same amount of sieved cocoa and then add a 100g packet of plain chocolate chips and a 100g packet of white chocolate chips. Mix together and divide the mixture between the muffin cases.

Right
Lemon Victoria Sandwich

BLUEBERRY MUFFINS
Stir 150g (5$\frac{1}{2}$ oz) of fresh or dried blueberries into the basic mixture.

CHRISTMAS MUFFINS
Take the basic muffin recipe and place half the mixture in the muffin cases then add a good teaspoon of mincemeat, top with the remaining muffin mixture.

CARROT AND CRANBERRY MUFFINS

These muffins originate from a tie-up with Farmhouse Breakfast Week, a national initiative to give us a good start to the day. They are a rich source of vitamin A, low in fat and taste delicious.

MAKES 6 LARGE MUFFINS OR 24 MINI MUFFINS
75g (3oz) carrots, peeled and finely grated
115g (4oz) wholemeal flour
25g (1oz) wheatgerm
2 level tsp baking powder

$\frac{1}{2}$ level tsp cinnamon
55g (2 oz) light soft brown sugar
50ml (2 fl oz) semi-skimmed milk
50ml (2 fl oz) sunflower oil
l egg, beaten
55g (2oz) cranberries

Place the grated carrot into a large bowl and stir in the flour, wheatgerm, baking powder, cinnamon and sugar. Gradually add the milk and oil followed by the egg and cranberries. Mix together. Divide the mixture between 6 muffin tins or 24 mini muffin tins.

MAIN OVEN 200°C (400°F), GAS MARK 6
Bake for about 20 minutes in the centre of the oven until they have risen. To test if they are cooked, insert a skewer into the centre of the muffin, it should come out clean. Serve warm.

SCONE FACTORY
SWEET SCONES

MAKES 9
225g (8 oz) self raising flour
$\frac{1}{2}$ tsp baking powder
25g (1 oz) butter
25g (1 oz) caster sugar
150ml ($\frac{1}{4}$ pint) milk
Glaze
Beaten egg or milk

Place the flour and baking powder into a basin and mix well together. Rub the butter into the flour until it resembles breadcrumbs. Stir in the sugar. Mix together to a soft dough with the milk.

Roll out to 1cm ($\frac{1}{2}$ inch) thick and cut out circles. Place on the plain shelf and brush with a little egg or milk.

MAIN OVEN 220°C (425°F), GAS MARK 7
Bake on the second runners down in the Main Oven for 8-10 minutes, until risen and golden. Turn the shelf once after 5 minutes.

Cool and serve the same day with clotted cream and jam.

TIP! These scones can be frozen after cooling. To thaw, place next to a warm Rayburn for 30 minutes.

VARIATIONS
• Add 55g (2 oz) sultanas.
• Add 55g (2 oz) cranberries.
• Add 25-55g (1-2 oz) mixed peel.

CHEESE SCONES

MAKES 8 TRIANGLES
225g (8 oz) self raising flour
1 tsp baking powder
85g (3 oz) butter
85g (3 oz) strong Cheddar cheese, grated
1 tsp dry mustard
A pinch of salt
1 egg
Milk or buttermilk to mix
Glaze
Beaten egg or milk

Right
Blueberry Muffins

Place the flour and baking powder into a basin and rub in the butter. Stir in the grated cheese and seasonings. Beat the egg and add with enough milk to make soft dough. Turn onto a floured surface and knead lightly. Roll out to about 1cm ($^1/_2$ inch) thick and cut into wedges or triangles. Place the scones onto a piece of Bake-O-Glide on the plain shelf.

MAIN OVEN 220°C (425°F), GAS MARK 7
Bake on the second runners down in the Main Oven for 8-10 minutes, until risen and golden. Turn the shelf once after 5 minutes.

Serve warm with butter or cream cheese.

VARIATIONS
- Add 25g (1oz) pumpkin seeds to the flour before adding the egg and milk.
- Substitute 85g (3 oz) goats' cheese for the Cheddar.
- These scones can also be made with wholemeal flour, or half wholemeal and half white flour. Add an extra teaspoon of baking powder.

TROPICAL TEA LOAF

MAKES 1 X 2 LB LOAF
115g (4 oz) dried chopped apricots
115g (4 oz) crystallised papaya, diced
115g (4 oz) chopped dates
115g (4 oz) brown sugar
115g (4 oz) Demerara sugar
115g (4 oz) Brazil nuts, halved
300ml ($^1/_2$ pint) hot tea
1 egg, beaten
280g (10 oz) wholemeal self raising flour

Soak the dried fruits, sugars and Brazil nuts in the hot tea overnight. Then stir in the egg and flour and turn into a prepared 900g (2 lb) loaf tin.

MAIN OVEN 180°C (350°F), GAS MARK 4
Bake on the oven grid shelf on the fourth runner down for about 65 minutes or until risen and cooked through.

Cool in the tin for 10 minutes then remove to cool completely on a wire rack. Serve sliced with or without butter – a personal choice!

SIMPLE TEA LOAF

MAKES 1 X 2 LB LOAF
350g (12 oz) dried fruit
225g (8 oz) brown sugar
300ml ($^1/_2$ pint) hot tea
1 egg, beaten
280g (10 oz) wholemeal self raising flour

Follow the method and cooking directions for the Tropical Tea Loaf, above.

CARWEN'S WELSH CAKES

MAKES 20
225g (8 oz) plain flour
1 tsp baking powder
$^1/_4$ tsp mixed spice
55g (2 oz) butter
55g (2 oz) lard or white fat
85g (3 oz) caster sugar
85g (3 oz) currants
1 egg, beaten
2-3 tbsp milk

Sift the flour, baking powder and spice together, and then rub in the fats until the mixture resembles breadcrumbs. Mix in the sugar and currants.
Add the egg and enough milk to make a stiff dough.

Roll out to about $^1/_2$ cm ($^1/_4$ inch) thick and cut into rounds.

HOTPLATE
Lightly oil the simmering to moderate side of the hotplate and cook the Welsh cakes until golden brown, about 4 minutes on each side.

Serve hot with butter.

CHERRY AND ALMOND COOKIES

You can buy blanched almonds already chopped, they are also known as nibbed almonds.

MAKES 40
225g (8 oz) butter, softened

115g (4 oz) caster sugar
280g (10 oz) self raising flour
Grated zest of 1 lemon
25g (1 oz) glacé cherries, chopped
25g (1 oz) blanched almonds, chopped

Cream the butter and sugar together until light and creamy. Add the flour, lemon zest, cherries and nuts. Work into a stiff paste. Divide the mixture into walnut-sized pieces and place them on greased baking trays or use Bake-O-Glide. Press the mixture down with the prongs of a fork.

MAIN OVEN 180°C (350°F), GAS MARK 4
Cook the cookies in the centre of the oven for 12-15 minutes until golden, turning the tray once if necessary to ensure even browning.

Remove the tray from the oven and allow 5 minutes to cool slightly before transferring to a wire rack to cool.

CHOCOLATE CHIP AND MACADAMIA COOKIES

MAKES 16-20
85g (3 oz) softened butter
115g (4 oz) caster sugar
55g (2 oz) light soft brown sugar
$^1/_2$ tsp vanilla extract
1 egg, beaten
175g (6 oz) self raising flour
60g (2$^1/_4$ oz) macadamia nuts, chopped
55g (2 oz) white chocolate chips
55g (2 oz) plain chocolate chips

Cream the butter and sugars together. Gradually beat in the vanilla and egg. Fold in the flour, nuts and chocolate chips.

Spoon tablespoonfuls of the mixture onto greased baking sheets, leaving room for each cookie to spread.

MAIN OVEN 180°C (350°F), GAS MARK 4
Bake in the centre of the oven for about 15 minutes or until golden brown. Turn the baking sheet halfway during cooking.

Cool on the tray for a couple of minutes before transferring to a wire rack.

FLORENTINES

MAKES 16
85g (3 oz) butter
85g (3 oz) golden syrup
25g (1 oz) plain flour
85g (3 oz) flaked almonds
25g (1 oz) chopped mixed peel
55g (2 oz) glacé cherries
1 tsp lemon juice

Melt the butter and syrup together in a saucepan. Remove from the heat and add the flour, almonds, peel, cherries and lemon juice. Mix well. Place a sheet of Bake-O-Glide on a baking sheet and put teaspoons of the mixture on to this, spaced well apart.

MAIN OVEN 180°C (350°F), GAS MARK 4
Cook at for about 8-10 minutes in the centre of the oven.

Shape into circles as soon as they come out of the oven with a cutter. Allow to cool and lift off onto a cooling rack.

VARIATION
• Delicious also with a chocolate base; spread the bases of the Florentines with melted chocolate, either plain, milk or white and allow to cool.

NAIN'S GINGER FAIRINGS

MAKES 24
175g (6 oz) self raising flour
1 level tsp bicarbonate of soda
2 level tsp ground ginger
115g (4 oz) caster sugar
55g (2 oz) vegetable shortening
1 scant tbsp golden syrup
1 medium egg, beaten

Sift the flour, bicarbonate of soda and ginger into a bowl and add the sugar. Melt the shortening and syrup and allow to cool a little before adding to the dry ingredients with the egg. Mix to a soft dough and divide into 24 pieces, rolling each into a ball. Place well apart on Bake-O-Glide or baking parchment on two baking trays.

MAIN OVEN 180°C (350°F), GAS MARK 4
Bake the trays on grid shelves on the second and fourth sets of runners. Cook for about 20 minutes, swapping the trays once, until a rich brown colour.

TRADITIONAL RICH FRUIT CAKE

Quantities are for a 20cm (8 inch) round cake tin or an 18cm (7 inch) square tin. It's recommended the tin has a solid base and is not loose-based. Cooking slowly means the cake remains flat for easy icing. *See the chart, opposite, for other tin size recipe quantities.*

SERVES 8-10
200g (7 oz) plain flour
1 tsp mixed ground spice
1/2 tsp freshly grated nutmeg
175g (6 oz) butter
175g (6 oz) muscovado sugar
Grated zest of 1 lemon
4 large eggs, beaten
55g (2 oz) ground almonds
280g (10 oz) currants
200g (7 oz) sultanas
115g (4 oz) raisins
85g (3 oz) glacé cherries
85g (3 oz) mixed peel, chopped
85g (3 oz) almonds, chopped
3 tbsp brandy

Grease and line, with a double thickness of baking parchment, a 20cm (8 inch) round cake tin or an 18cm (7 inch) square cake tin.

Sieve the flour and the spices together. Cream the butter and sugar until light and fluffy, beat in the finely grated lemon zest.

Gradually beat in the eggs, which should be at room temperature, adding a tablespoon of flour towards the end, to prevent curdling. Fold in the remaining flour, ground almonds, fruit and nuts until thoroughly mixed. Turn the mixture into the prepared tin and smooth the top.

MAIN OVEN 140°C (275°F), GAS MARK 1
Place the cake tin on the grid shelf on the lowest set of runners. Bake for about 5-6 hours until cooked. If the top is browned to your liking but the cake is not cooked put a piece of foil or greaseproof paper over the top of the cake. Test with a skewer; if a skewer inserted into the centre of the cake comes out clean, it is cooked. Or if the cake has stopped 'singing' this is also an indication of being done.

Leave in the tin for 30 minutes and then turn onto a wire rack to cool. Prick the surface of the cake with a skewer and spoon the brandy over. Wrap in foil until required. Decorate with almond paste and royal icing.

This size cake will need 675g (1 1/2 lb) of almond paste to cover and the same amount of royal icing – 3 egg whites to 675g (1 1/2 lb) icing sugar.

VARIATION
Instead of covering with almond paste and royal icing, try a nut and cherry topping. Before the cake goes into the oven, place Brazil nuts, walnut halves and glacé cherries in a pattern on the top of the cake. When the cake is cooked brush the topping with an apricot glaze.

SHORTBREAD

Beloved by people all over the world, shortbread must be 'the' ambassador for Scotland. There are several recipes and many a discussion of whether to add rice flour or cornflour. This is our favourite and most used recipe that uses neither! If you are of the school that prefers more of a bite, then substitute rice flour or cornflour for a quarter of the flour.

MAKES 12 TRIANGLES
175g (6 oz) butter
55g (2 oz) caster sugar
225g (8 oz) plain flour
Extra caster sugar to finish

Cream the butter and sugar together and stir in the flour. Use your hand to pull the dough together into a ball and divide in two.

Roll out each portion into two circles about 15cm (6 in) in diameter. Place on the plain shelf or on two baking sheets. Then crimp the edges of each circle and mark into six sections. Prick with a fork.

MAIN OVEN 180°C (350°F), GAS MARK 4
Cook in the centre of the oven for about 20 minutes until a light golden colour.

Remove the shortbread from the oven and immediately cut into six portions, using the marks made before cooking. Sprinkle with caster sugar. Allow to cool for 10 minutes. Remove to a cooling rack and allow to go cold.

VARIATIONS
• For orange shortbread: grate the zest of one orange into the creamed butter and sugar.

QUANTITIES FOR RICH FRUIT CAKES
Note: for the 20cm (8 inch) round cake see the recipe opposite

ROUND	15cm (6inch)	18cm (7inch)	23cm (9inch)	25cm (10inch)	28cm (11inch)	30cm (12inch)
SQUARE	13cm (5inch)	15cm (6inch)	20cm (8inch)	23cm (9inch)	25cm (10inch)	28cm (11inch)
Plain flour	115g (4 oz)	175g (6 oz)	250g (9 oz)	325g (11 oz)	400g (14 oz)	450g (1 lb)
Ground mixed spice	$\frac{1}{2}$ teaspoon	$\frac{1}{2}$ teaspoon	$1\frac{1}{2}$ teaspoons	2 teaspoons	2 teaspoons	2 teaspoons
Ground nutmeg	$\frac{1}{4}$ teaspoon	$\frac{1}{2}$ teaspoon	$\frac{1}{2}$ teaspoon	$\frac{1}{2}$ teaspoon	$\frac{1}{2}$ teaspoon	1 teaspoon
Butter	100g ($3\frac{1}{2}$ oz)	140g (5 oz)	225g (8 oz)	300g (10 oz)	350g (12 oz)	400g (14 oz)
Muscovado sugar	100g ($3\frac{1}{2}$ oz)	140g (5 oz)	225g (8 oz)	300g (10 oz)	350g (12 oz)	400g (14 oz)
Grated lemon zest	$\frac{1}{2}$ lemon	1 lemon	1 lemon	1 lemon	2 lemons	2 lemons
Eggs	2 large	3 large	5 large	6 large	7 large	8 large
Ground almonds	25g (1 oz)	40g ($1\frac{1}{2}$ oz)	70g ($2\frac{1}{2}$ oz)	85g (3 oz)	100g ($3\frac{1}{2}$ oz)	115g (4 oz)
Currants	175g (6 oz)	225g (8 oz)	375g (13 oz)	450g (1 lb)	550g ($1\frac{1}{4}$ lb)	675g ($1\frac{1}{2}$ lb)
Sultanas	115g (4 oz)	140g (5 oz)	250g (9 oz)	325g (11 oz)	375g (13 oz)	450g (1 lb)
Raisins	55g (2 oz)	85g (3 oz)	140g (5 oz)	175g (6 oz)	200g (7 oz)	225g (8 oz)
Glacé cherries	40g ($1\frac{1}{2}$ oz)	55g (2 oz)	100g ($3\frac{1}{2}$ oz)	115g (4 oz)	140g (5 oz)	175g (6 oz)
Mixed peel	40g ($1\frac{1}{2}$ oz)	55g (2 oz)	100g ($3\frac{1}{2}$ oz)	115g (4 oz)	140g (5 oz)	175g (6 oz)
Blanched almonds	40g ($1\frac{1}{2}$ oz)	55g (2 oz)	100g ($3\frac{1}{2}$ oz)	115g (4 oz)	140g (5 oz)	175g (6 oz)
Brandy	2 tablespoons	2 tablespoons	3 tablespoons	4 tablespoons	4 tablespoons	5 tablespoons

QUANTITIES FOR ALMOND PASTE AND ROYAL ICING

Almond paste and Royal icing	350g (12 oz)	450g (1 lb)	900g (2 lb)	1.1kg ($2\frac{1}{2}$ lb)	1.3kg (3 lb)	1.6kg ($3\frac{1}{2}$ lb)

- For lemon shortbread: grate the zest of one lemon into the creamed butter and sugar.
- For cinnamon shortbread: add $1/2$-1 teaspoon of cinnamon to the creamed butter and sugar.
- For ginger shortbread: add 1 teaspoon of ground ginger to the creamed butter and sugar. Decorate the top with pieces of crystallised or glacé ginger.

CHOCOLATE SHORTBREAD BISCUITS

55g (2 oz) dark chocolate chips
55g (2 oz) white chocolate chips
2 paper piping bags
Shortbread Mixture (see previous page)

Put the dark chocolate chips into a piping bag, making sure the tip is well sealed. Do the same with the white chocolate chips. Place the piping bags at the back of the Rayburn top plate to melt – this method means there is no need to melt the chocolate over a pan of hot water, the gentle warmth of the Rayburn does it all for you.

Make up the shortbread and roll out, use a cutter to cut into shapes. Bake as before. Allow to cool. Snip off the points of the piping bags and decorate the shortbread biscuits with a lattice of the melted chocolate.

DATE, WALNUT AND ORANGE FLAPJACK

MAKES 48 SQUARES
250g (9 oz) butter
250g (9 oz) light brown sugar
250g (9 oz) golden syrup
500g (1 lb 1 oz) rolled oats
85g (3 oz) walnut pieces
115g (4 oz) chopped dates
Grated zest of 1 orange

Melt the butter, sugar and syrup in a large pan. Remove from the heat and stir in the oats, walnuts, dates and orange zest. Divide the mixture between two Swiss roll tins, 18cm x 28cm (7 inch x 11 inch). Press down the mixture.

MAIN OVEN 180°C (350°F), GAS MARK 4
Place one tray on the fourth runner and the other on the fourth runner. Bake for about 20 minutes, until golden, swap the trays over half way through cooking.

Mark into squares, whilst hot. Allow to cool. Remove from the tins and cut into squares.

VARIATION
- Substitute the walnuts, dates and orange rind with 115g (4 oz) chopped apricots, 1 tsp ground ginger and 85g (3 oz) chopped glacé ginger.

NAAN BREADS

This recipe was given to us by a chef (hence the large quantities), however, making this amount means some can be frozen to be used later.

1.5kg (3 lb 5 oz) strong plain flour
15g ($1/2$ oz) salt
15g ($1/2$ oz) baking powder
55g (2 oz) fresh yeast
450ml (16 fl oz) milk
150ml ($1/4$ pint) vegetable oil
450ml (16 fl oz) plain yoghurt

Mix the flour, salt and baking powder together. Cream the yeast with a little milk. Mix the oil, milk and yoghurt together and add, together with the yeast to the dry ingredients. Combine and knead until smooth.

Divide the mixture into rolls and allow to prove. Roll out.

HOTPLATE
Have the hotplate at maximum setting. Cook both sides of the naans on the simmering side of the hotplate, which should be lightly oiled. Then finish on the hottest side for just a few seconds either side for that authentic look.

Right
Date, Walnut and Orange Flapjack

FLOWER POT LOAVES

An unusual way of presenting a loaf using terracotta flower pots as the cooking vessels. The pots need to be treated before using. Thoroughly oil the inside of clean new terracotta flower pots and place empty into a hot oven, 200°C (400°F), Gas Mark 6, for 15 minutes, repeat this process for 3 or 4 times to season them.

350g (12 oz) wholemeal flour
350g (12 oz) strong plain white flour
1 sachet of easy blend yeast
2 tsp salt
15g ($^1/_2$ oz) butter
450ml ($^3/_4$ pint) warm water
Glaze
Beaten egg mixed with 1 tbsp milk and a pinch of salt
Topping
Poppy, pumpkin, sesame or fennel seeds

Place the two flours into a large bowl and mix together, add the yeast and salt and mix in. Make a well in the centre, add the butter then add the water. Work the butter into the water until it has melted, and then combine the flour and the liquid.

Knead for 10 minutes. Leave to rest for 5 minutes, covered with cling film, or a damp cloth.

Knead again and divide between your chosen sizes of terracotta pots – allowing enough dough to half-fill each pot. Cover the flower pot and place next to the Rayburn to prove, until doubled in size. Remove the covering. Brush the tops with the egg glaze and sprinkle with the chosen topping.

MAIN OVEN 200°C (400°F), GAS MARK 6
Bake on the grid shelf on the fourth set of runners for 25-40 minutes, dependent upon the size of the pots. To test for doneness, tap the loaves, they should sound hollow.

TIP! This recipe will make 16 bread rolls, or 2 x 450g (1 lb) loaf tins or 1 x 900g (2 lb) loaf tin.

VARIATIONS
• For Herb Bread add 3 tbsp chopped fresh mixed herbs before adding the water.
• Olive and Tomato Bread – add 85g (3 oz) each of pitted black sliced olives and halved sun dried tomatoes, before adding the water.

• Onion and Cheese Bread – add 1 chopped onion (sautéed in butter until golden) with 140g (5 oz) of grated mature Cheddar cheese and 1 tsp of mustard powder, before adding the water.

SELKIRK BANNOCK

Not a bread roll, but a highly fruited, rich yeast bread.

450g (1 lb) strong plain flour
$^1/_2$ tsp salt
85g (3 oz) caster sugar
250ml (9 fl oz) milk
15g ($^1/_2$ oz) fresh yeast
55g (2 oz) butter
55g (2 oz) lard
225g (8 oz) sultanas
55g (2 oz) mixed peel
Beaten egg to glaze

Place the flour, salt and sugar into a bowl and put by the Rayburn to warm. Warm the milk until tepid on the simmering side of the hotplate. Take a little of this tepid milk and mix with the yeast, put to one side. Slowly melt the butter and lard, do not over heat.

Make a well in the flour and pour in the milk and melted fats, then add the yeast and mix well to a smooth dough. Cover the bowl with cling film and leave by the warm Rayburn until doubled in size, about $1^1/_2$-$1^3/_4$ hours. Remove the dough from the bowl, add the sultanas and mixed peel, knead for 5 minutes. Shape into a round loaf and place onto a circle of Bake-O-Glide set on a baking sheet. Cover with a large oiled plastic bag and set near the Rayburn to prove, until about doubled in size – test by prodding with your finger, the dough should spring back. Brush with a little beaten egg.

MAIN OVEN AT 190°C (375°F), GAS MARK 5
Place the baking sheet on the oven grid shelf on the fourth set of runners down and bake for about 45-50 minutes, until browned and cooked through. If the top is over-browning, slide in the cold plain shelf above the bannock.

Remove from the oven and place on a wire rack to cool. Serve thinly sliced, spread with butter or, for a change, a soft Scottish cheese.

Right
Flower Pot Loaves

HOME PRESERVING

Due to the large capacity of the Rayburn, home preserving becomes much simpler. The sugar can be placed in the meat tin and pre-heated in the Main Oven and the jars safely left in the Lower Oven to sterilise.
It's essential to use a pan with a suitable base to get the best results when boiling mixtures for a set (*see* p14). We think it's easier to make several smaller batches of jam or marmalade at a time, than to try and tackle larger quantities.

EASY MARMALADE

MAKES ABOUT 2.25 KG (5 LBS)
750g (1¹/₂ lbs) Seville oranges
Juice of 2 large lemons
2 litres (4 pints) water
1.4 kg (3 lb) granulated sugar

Wash the fruit, cut in half and place in a large pan with the lemon juice and water. Cover the fruit with an enamelled or Pyrex plate to keep it submerged. Bring to the boil on the boiling end of the hotplate.

MAIN OVEN 120°C (250°F), GAS MARK L-1
Cover and transfer to the floor of the oven and cook overnight. Place jars on a metal tray ready for warming in the oven. Measure out the sugar and put into the meat tin, place the tin on a cloth on top of one of the closed lids.

In the morning, remove the pan from the oven and take off the lid and allow the contents to cool down. Turn the cooker to its highest setting ready for the sugar boiling and place the sugar in the Lower Oven to warm. Cut up the fruit, thinly, reserving the pips. Add the pips to the liquid in the pan and bring to the boil for 5 minutes. Strain the liquid through a nylon sieve and return to the rinsed pan with the fruit.

Heat on the simmering end of the hotplate and when just simmering, add the warm sugar. Place the tray of jars in the Lower Oven to heat through. When the sugar has completely dissolved, move the pan to the boiling end of the hotplate and boil rapidly until setting point is reached (15-20 minutes). Remove from the heat and leave to stand for 10-15 minutes before potting in the hot jars. Cover and seal in the usual way.

BRAMBLE JELLY

MAKES ABOUT 1.8KG (4 LBS)
2kg (4 lb) blackberries, firm and just ripe,
*   and a handful of red under-ripe berries*
1 level tsp citric acid
600ml (1 pint) water
Granulated sugar

Rinse the fruit quickly in a colander, then put into a large pan with the acid. Add the water and stir and crush the fruit with a masher and wooden spoon whilst heating it to simmering point on the hotplate. Simmer on the simmering end of the hotplate for 30 minutes, until very soft. Strain through a jelly bag (or use several layers of muslin) overnight. Do not press the pulp but just allow the juice to drip naturally. Measure the juice, and allow 400g (1 lb) of granulated sugar to each 500ml (1 pint) juice.

Put the sugar into the meat tin and place in the Lower Oven to warm. Turn the cooker to its highest setting ready for boiling for a set. Have ready a metal oven tray with small glass jars. In a clean pan, bring the measured juice to the boil on the simmering end of the hotplate. Remove the warmed sugar from the oven and add to the hot liquid. Place the jars in the Lower Oven at this point to heat through. Stir frequently, when the sugar is fully dissolved, move the pan to the boiling end of the hotplate. Boil rapidly until the jelly will set on testing. Pot immediately into the hot jars, cover and seal them.

APPLE AND MINT JELLY

MAKES ABOUT 1.8KG (4 LBS)
2kg (4 lb) green cooking apples or *crab apples*
Granulated sugar
2-3 sprays of mint
1 litre (2 pints) water
150ml (5 fl oz) dry cider
2 tbsp white wine vinegar
A good handful of fresh mint
A few drops of natural green food colouring (optional)

Wash the apples, cut them into pieces and put them into a large pan. If you're using windfalls make sure you remove any bruises. Add two or three sprays of mint, pour in the water with the cider and wine vinegar to barely cover the fruit. Place on the boiling end of the hotplate then simmer on the hotplate for 5 minutes.

MAIN OVEN 120°C (250°F), GAS MARK L-1
Cover and transfer to the floor of the oven for 45-60 minutes, until very soft. Strain through a jelly bag (or several layers of muslin) overnight. Do not press the pulp but just allow the juice to drip naturally. Measure the juice back into the cleaned pan, and allow 400g (1 lb) of granulated sugar to each 500ml (1 pint) juice. Place the sugar into the meat tin and place in the Lower Oven to warm.

Turn the cooker to its highest setting ready for boiling for a set. Have ready a metal oven tray with small glass jars. Bring the measured juice to the boil on the simmering end of the hotplate. Remove the warmed sugar from the oven and add to the hot liquid. Place the jars in the

Lower Oven at this point to heat through. Finely chop 2-3 tablespoons of the youngest mint leaves. When the sugar is fully dissolved, move the pan to the boiling end of the hotplate and boil the jelly rapidly for 5 minutes, then test for a set and repeat every couple of minutes until a set is obtained. Take the pan from the heat, skim quickly and then add the finely chopped mint and colouring, if using. Pot immediately into the hot jars, cover and seal them.

LEMON CURD

MAKES ABOUT 675G (1$^1/_2$ LBS)
85g (3 oz) butter
225g (8 oz) caster sugar
2 large unwaxed lemons
2 whole eggs or 4 egg yolks

Measure the butter and sugar into a Pyrex bowl and place over a small pan of simmering water. Do not allow the water to touch the base of the bowl. Remove the rind from the lemons and when the butter has melted, add together with the juice. (Placing the lemons in the oven for a few minutes will help extract the most juice.) Stir well and when the sugar has almost dissolved, add the eggs or yolks and mix well. Continue to cook for 25-30 minutes until the mixture thickens, stirring every few minutes. Warm the jars in the Lower Oven and pot quickly. Store in the refrigerator for up to a month.

RASPBERRY JAM

MAKES ABOUT 3 KG (7 LBS)
2kg (4$^1/_2$ lb) firm and just ripe raspberries
2kg (4$^1/_2$ lb) granulated sugar
Juice of 1 lemon

Turn the cooker to its highest setting. Place the sugar in a meat tin and place in the Lower Oven to warm through for 15 minutes before it is needed. Place the fruit in a large pan. Lightly crush some of the fruit with a masher and add the warmed sugar with the lemon juice. Place the pan on the simmering end of the hotplate and heat gently, stirring slowly to draw the juice and dissolve the sugar. When the sugar has completely dissolved, move the pan to the boiling end of the hotplate and bring to a good rolling boil. Place the jars to warm in the Lower Oven. Test for the setting point every couple of minutes in the normal way. Remove from the heat and pot into the hot jars, cover and seal.

STRAWBERRY PRESERVE

MAKES ABOUT 3 KG (7 LBS)
2kg (4$^1/_2$ lb) small or Alpine strawberries
2kg (4$^1/_2$ lb) granulated sugar
4 tbsp lemon juice

Hull the berries and layer them in a large bowl with the sugar. Cover and leave overnight to extract the juice and firm the berries. In the morning, turn the cooker to its highest setting. Place the fruit and sugar into a large pan with the lemon juice, and heat on the simmering end of the hotplate until a slow boil is reached. Maintain this for 5-6 minutes. Leave to cool then return the mixture to the bowl for 12 hours, boil again gently until the syrup thickens somewhat. Place the jars to warm in the Lower Oven. Stir carefully to avoid breaking up the fruit. Allow to stand for 10 minutes before potting into hot jars to ensure even distribution of fruit.

GOOSEBERRY JAM

MAKES ABOUT 2.25 KG (5 LBS)
2kg (4$^1/_2$ lbs) gooseberries
2.5kg (5 lbs) granulated sugar
700ml (1$^1/_4$ pints) water
6 sprays of just open elderflowers (if available)

Wash and top and tail the gooseberries. Place in a large pan with the water and bring to the boil on the boiling end of the hotplate. Move to the simmering end of the hotplate and simmer gently until the skins are very tender. If using, shake the elderflowers well, rinse and tie in a piece of butter muslin; tie the bag to the pan handle and push the bag well down into the water before simmering the fruit.

Place the sugar in a meat tin in the Lower Oven to warm through. Add the sugar to the fruit. Place the jars to warm in the Lower Oven at this point. Stir the mixture until the sugar is completely dissolved, then move to the boiling end of the hotplate and boil rapidly. As the jam begins to thicken, remove the bag of elderflowers, pressing it against the side of the pan with a spoon. Test for setting in the usual way, every few minutes, (gooseberry has good levels of pectin and sets easily). Pot immediately into the hot jars, cover and seal them.

Right
Lemon Curd

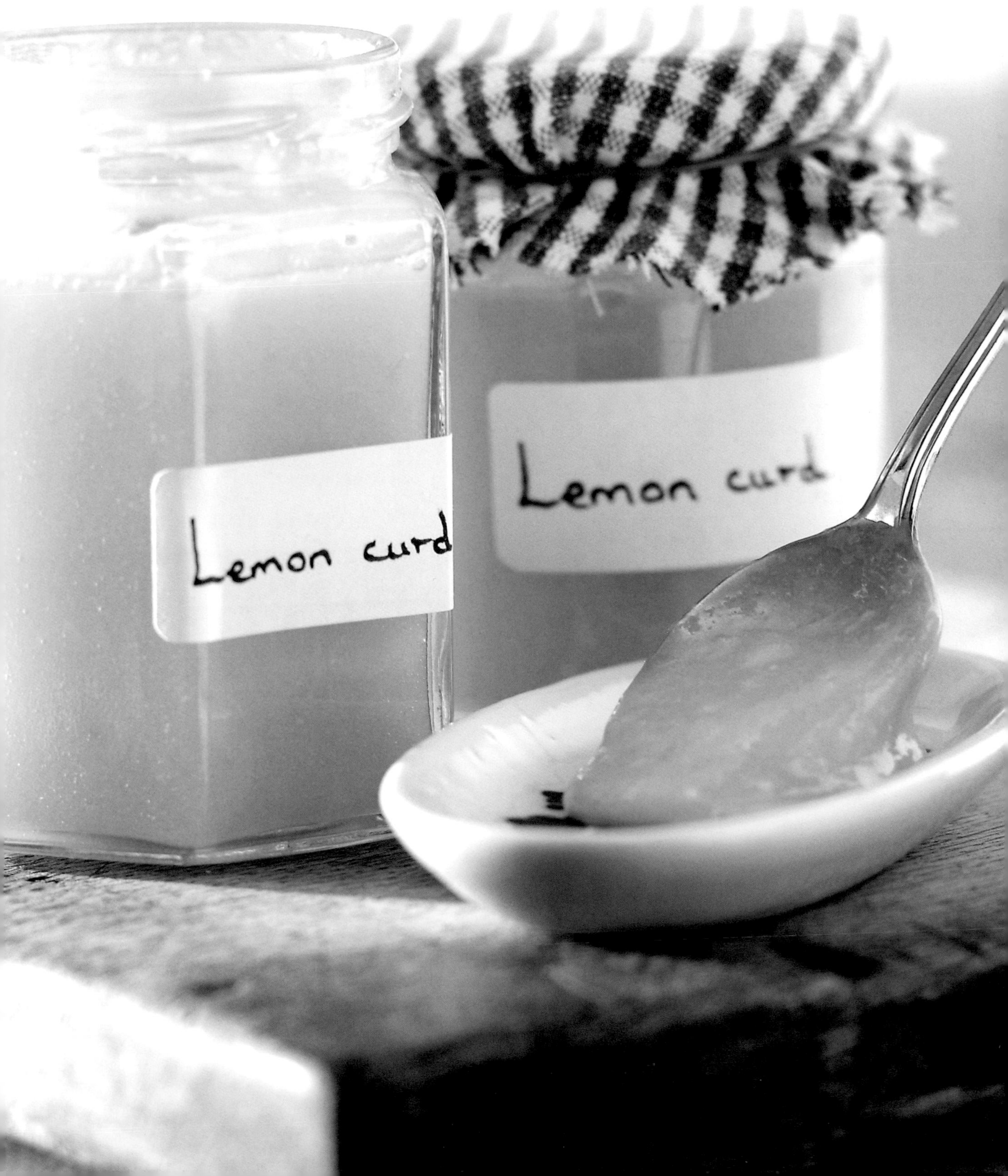
Lemon curd
Lemon curd

INDEX

ACKNOWLEDGEMENTS

Our thanks to all our colleagues, friends, family, fellow cooks and, of course, Rayburn owners everywhere for their constant support and encouragement. A special thanks to the Rayburn demonstrator network for their suggestions and testing of recipes. To everyone at Aga – who make the Rayburn – thank you for your support, comments and taste testing, it is a pleasure to continue to work with such an enthusiastic group of people across the company. Also, a huge thank you to our publisher, Jon Croft, editor Meg Avent and graphic designer Matt Inwood at Absolute Press who are the best people in the world to write a book with. They have helped make this book a pleasure to write.

RAYBURN is a registered trademark of Aga Foodservice Group plc.
BAKE-O-GLIDE™ is a re-usable non-stick coated cooking material, available from all Aga and Rayburn Stockists.

SOME USEFUL WEBSITES
www.aga-rayburn.co.uk
www.agalinks.com
www.agacookshop.co.uk
www.agafoodservice.com

RICHARD MAGGS
A dynamic and accomplished chef, Richard is an authority on Aga and Rayburn cookery. As well as having featured on TV and radio, he writes for several magazines and contributes a regular column to the official Aga Magazine for Aga and Rayburn owners. A bestselling author, he has written many books on range cooking including *The Little Book of Rayburn Tips*. He is also the resident Aga and Rayburn cookery expert, The Cookery Doctor, with the award-winning Agalinks website at www.agalinks.com. This is his seventh book.

DAWN ROADS
As a trained and respected Home Economist with a love of good food, Dawn has long specialised in Aga and Rayburn cooking. She is Food Editor for *Aga Magazine* and is a consultant in the use and cooking on the Rayburn and Aga. She has owned both products at different times in her life. As well as featuring on TV, radio and in the media she was co-author of *A Lifetime of Aga*. She is also a contributor to the Agalinks website with articles and recipes

GENERAL COOKING CHART FOR THE MAIN OVEN

DISH	SETTING °C	SHELF POSITION	APPROXIMATE TIME
BAKED CUSTARD	150	4	1½ hours
BAKED FISH	190	3	15-20 minutes, dependent on size
BAKED POTATOES	230	Anywhere	1¼ hour
BISCUITS	180-190	2 or 3	10-15 minutes
BREAD (loaf)	230-240	5	30-35 minutes
BREAD (rolls)	230	3 or 4	15-20 minutes
CASSEROLES	140-150	3, 4 or 5	2-3 hours
CHOUX PASTRY	200	2, 3 or 4	20-30 minutes
GINGERBREAD	160	3	1-1¼ hours, dependent on recipe
QUICHE	200	Floor	30-40 minutes
MERINGUES	Low	5	1½-2¼ hours
MILK PUDDINGS	120	4	2 hours
PUFF PASTRY	230	2 or 3	10-15 minutes
RICH FRUIT CAKE	140	5	Depending on size (see page 131)
ROAST MEAT	180-230	Anywhere	See roasting page 43
ROAST POTATOES	230	Floor	30-45 minutes
SCONES	220	2	10-15 minutes
SHORTCRUST PASTRY	200	2, 3 or 4	20-40 minutes, dependent on recipe
SEMI-RICH FRUIT CAKE	150-160	5	1½-2 hours
SMALL CAKES	190	3	20 minutes
SOUFFLES	190	4	25-35 minutes
SOUP OR STOCK	120	Anywhere	2-3 hours
SPONGES (fatless)	200	4 or 5	8-25 minutes, dependent on recipe
VICTORIA SANDWICH	180	3 and 5	18-25 minutes, interchange tins
YORKSHIRE PUDDING	220	2 or 3	25-35 minutes

SHELF POSITIONS ARE COUNTED DOWNWARDS FROM THE TOP OF THE MAIN OVEN.
THE POSITIONS ARE A GUIDE ONLY AND, OF COURSE, CAN BE ALTERED.
TIMINGS ARE A GENERALISATION – FOR SPECIFIC RECIPES FOLLOW THE INSTRUCTION.